TOSEL ®

Basic

Listening

CONTENTS

INTRO

Basic

TOSEL® Level Chart   TOSEL 단계표

COCOON
아이들이 접할 수 있는 공식 인증 시험의 첫 단계로써, 아이들의 부담을 줄이고 즐겁게 흥미를 유발할 수 있도록 컬러풀한 색상과 디자인으로 시험지를 구성하였습니다.

Pre-STARTER
친숙한 주제에 대한 단어, 짧은 대화, 짧은 문장을 사용한 기본적인 문장표현 능력을 측정합니다.

STARTER
흔히 접할 수 있는 주제와 상황과 관련된 주제에 대한 짧은 대화 및 짧은 문장을 이해하고 일상생활 대화에 참여하며 실질적인 영어 기초 의사소통 능력을 측정합니다.

BASIC
개인 정보와 일상 활동, 미래 계획, 과거의 경험에 대해 구어와 문어의 형태로 의사소통을 할 수 있는 능력을 측정합니다.

JUNIOR
일반적인 주제와 상황을 다루는 회화와 짧은 단락, 실용문, 짧은 연설 등을 이해하고 간단한 일상 대화에 참여하는 능력을 측정합니다.

HIGH JUNIOR
넓은 범위의 사회적, 학문적 주제에서 영어를 유창하고 정확하게, 효과적으로 사용할 수 있는 능력 및 중문과 복잡한 문장을 포함한 다양한 문장구조의 사용 능력을 측정합니다.

ADVANCED
대학 및 대학원에서 요구되는 영어능력과 취업 또는 직업근무환경에 필요한 실용영어 능력을 측정합니다.

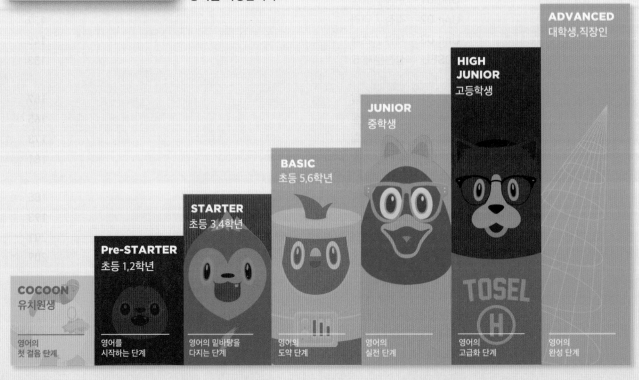

COCOON 유치원생 — 영어의 첫 걸음 단계

Pre-STARTER 초등 1,2학년 — 영어를 시작하는 단계

STARTER 초등 3,4학년 — 영어의 밑바탕을 다지는 단계

BASIC 초등 5,6학년 — 영어의 도약 단계

JUNIOR 중학생 — 영어의 실전 단계

HIGH JUNIOR 고등학생 — 영어의 고급화 단계

ADVANCED 대학생,직장인 — 영어의 완성 단계

TOSEL
교재 Series

TOSEL LEVEL	Age	Vocabulary Frequency	Readability Score	교과 과정 연계	Listening	VOCA	Reading	Grammar
Cocoon	K5-K7	500	0-1	Who is he? (국어 1단원 1-1)	Phonics	150	Picking Pumpkins (Phonics Story)	There is . There are
Pre-Starter	P1-P2	700		How old are you? (통합교과 1-1)	묘사하기	300	Me & My Family (Reading series Ch.1)	be + adjective
Starter	P3-P4	1000-2000	1-2	Spring, Summer, Fall, Winter (통합교과 3-1)	날씨/시간 표현	800	Ask More Questions (Reading Series Ch.1)	Simple Present
Basic	P5-P6	3000-4000	3-4	Show and Tell (사회 5-1)	상대방 의견 묻고 답하기	1700	Culture (Reading Series Ch.3)	Superlative
Junior	M1-M2	5000-6000	5-6	중 1, 2 과학, 기술가정	정보 묻고 답하기	4000	Humans and Animals (Reading Series Ch.1)	to-infinitive
High Junior	H1-H3			고등학교 - 체육	사건 묘사하기	7000	Health (Reading Series Ch.1)	2nd Conditional

■ TOSEL의 세분화된 레벨은 각 연령에 맞는 어휘와 읽기 지능 및 교과 과정과의 연계가
가능하도록 설계된 교재들로 효과적인 학습 커리큘럼을 제공합니다.

■ TOSEL의 커리큘럼에 따른 학습은
정확한 레벨링 → 레벨에 적합한 학습 → 영어 능력 인증 시험 TOSEL에서의 공신력 있는 평가를 통해
진단 → 학습 → 평가의 선순환 구조를 실현합니다.

TOSEL은 각급 학교 교과과정과 연령별 인지단계를 고려하여 단계별 난이도와 문항으로
영어 숙달 정도를 측정하는 영어 사용자 중심의 맞춤식 영어능력인증 시험제도입니다.
평가유형에 따른 개인별 장점과 단점을 파악하고, 개인별 영어학습 방향을 제시하는 성적분석자료를 제공하여
영어능력 종합검진 서비스를 제공함으로써 영어 사용자인 소비자와
영어능력 평가를 토대로 영어교육을 담당하는 교사 및 기관 인사관리자인 공급자를
모두 만족시키는 영어능력인증 평가입니다.

TOSEL은 인지적-학문적 언어 사용의 유창성 (Cognitive-Academic Language Proficiency, CALP)과
기본적-개인적 의사소통능력 (Basic Interpersonal Communication Skill, BICS)을
엄밀히 구분하여 수험자의 언어능력을 가장 친밀하게 평가하는 시험입니다.

대상	목적	용도
유아, 초, 중, 고등학생, 대학생 및 직장인 등 성인	한국인의 영어구사능력 증진과 비영어권 국가의 영어 사용자의 영어구사능력 증진	실질적인 영어구사능력 평가 + 입학전형 및 인재선발 등에 활용 및 직무역량별 인재 배치

연혁

2002.02	국제토셀위원회 창설 (수능출제위원역임 전국대학 영어전공교수진 중심)
2004.09	TOSEL 고려대학교 국제어학원 공동인증시험 실시
2006.04	EBS 한국교육방송공사 주관기관 참여
2006.05	민족사관고등학교 입학전형에 반영
2008.12	고려대학교 편입학시험 TOSEL 유형으로 대체
2009.01	서울시 공무원 근무평정에 TOSEL 점수 가산점 부여
2009.01	전국 대부분 외고, 자사고 입학전형에 TOSEL 반영 (한영외국어고등학교, 한일고등학교, 고양외국어고등학교, 과천외국어고등학교, 김포외국어고등학교, 명지외국어고등학교, 부산국제외국어고등학교, 부일외국어 고등학교, 성남외국어고등학교, 인천외국어고등학교, 전북외국어고등학교, 대전외국어고등학교, 청주외국어고등학교, 강원외국어고등학교, 전남외국어고등학교)
2009.12	청심국제중・고등학교 입학전형 TOSEL 반영
2009.12	한국외국어교육학회, 팬코리아영어교육학회, 한국음성학회, 한국응용언어학회 TOSEL 인증
2010.03	고려대학교, TOSEL 출제기관 및 공동 인증기관으로 참여
2010.07	경찰청 공무원 임용 TOSEL 성적 가산점 부여
2014.04	전국 200개 초등학교 단체 응시 실시
2017.03	중앙일보 주관기관 참여
2018.11	관공서, 대기업 등 100여 개 기관에서 TOSEL 반영
2019.06	미얀마 TOSEL 도입 발족식 베트남 TOSEL 도입 협약식
2019.11	2020학년도 고려대학교 편입학전형 반영
2020.04	국토교통부 국가자격시험 TOSEL 반영
2021.07	소방청 간부후보생 선발시험 TOSEL 반영

About **TOSEL**®

What's TOSEL?

"Test of Skills in the English Language"

TOSEL은 비영어권 국가의 영어 사용자를 대상으로 영어구사능력을 측정하여
그 결과를 공식 인증하는 영어능력인증 시험제도입니다.

영어 사용자 중심의 맞춤식 영어능력 인증 시험제도

맞춤식 평가

획일적인 평가에서
세분화된 평가로의 전환

TOSEL은 응시자의 연령별 인지단계에
따라 별도의 문항과 난이도를 적용하여
평가함으로써 평가의 목적과 용도에
적합한 평가 시스템을
구축하였습니다.

공정성과 신뢰성 확보

국제토셀위원회의 역할

TOSEL은 고려대학교가 출제 및 인증기관
으로 참여하였고 대학입학수학능력시험
출제위원 교수들이 중심이 된
국제토셀위원회가 주관하여
사회적 공정성과 신뢰성을 확보한
평가 제도입니다.

수입대체 효과

외화유출 차단 및 국위선양

TOSEL은 해외시험응시로 인한 외화의
유출을 마는 수입대체외 효과를 기대할 수
있습니다. TOSEL의 문항과 시험제도는
비영어권 국가에 수출하여 국위선양에
기여하고 있습니다.

Why **TOSEL**® ——— 왜 TOSEL인가

01 학교 시험 폐지

일선 학교에서 중간, 기말고사 폐지로 인해 객관적인 영어 평가 제도의 부재가 우려됩니다. 그러나 전국단위로 연간 4번 시행되는 TOSEL 평가시험을 통해 학생들은 정확한 역량과 체계적인 학습방향을 꾸준히 진단받을 수 있습니다.

02 연령별/단계별 대비로 영어학습 점검

TOSEL은 응시자의 연령별 인지단계 및 영어 학습 단계에 따라 총 7단계로 구성되었습니다. 각 단계에 알맞은 문항유형과 난이도를 적용해 모든 연령 및 학습 과정에 맞추어 가장 효율적으로 영어실력을 평가할 수 있도록 개발된 영어시험입니다.

03 학교내신성적 향상

TOSEL은 학년별 교과과정과 연계하여 학교에서 배우는 내용을 학습하고 평가할 수 있도록 문항 및 주제를 구성하여 내신영어 향상을 위한 최적의 솔루션을 제공합니다.

04 수능대비 직결

유아, 초, 중등시절 어렵지 않고 즐겁게 학습해 온 영어이지만, 수능시험준비를 위해 접하는 영어의 문항 및 유형 난이도에 주춤하게 됩니다. 이를 대비하기 위해 TOSEL은 유아부터 성인까지 점진적인 학습을 통해 수능대비를 자연적으로 해나갈 수 있습니다.

05 진학과 취업에 대비한 필수 스펙관리

개인별 '학업성취기록부' 발급을 통해 영어학업성취이력을 꾸준히 기록한 영어학습 포트폴리오를 제공하여 영어학습 이력을 관리할 수 있습니다.

06 자기소개서에 토셀 기재

개별적인 진로 적성 Report를 제공하여 진로를 파악하고 자기소개서 작성시 적극적으로 활용할 수 있는 객관적인 자료를 제공합니다.

07 영어학습 동기부여

시험실시 후 응시자 모두에게 수여되는 인증서는 영어학습에 대한 자신감과 성취감을 고취시키고 동기를 부여합니다.

08 AI 분석 영어학습 솔루션

국내외 15,000여 개 학교·학원 단체 응시인원 중 엄선한 100만 명 이상의 실제 TOSEL 성적 데이터를 기반으로 영어인증시험 제도 중 세계 최초로 인공지능이 분석한 개인별 AI 정밀 진단 성적표를 제공합니다. 최첨단 AI 정밀진단 성적표는 최적의 영어 학습 솔루션을 제시하여 영어 학습에 소요되는 시간과 노력을 획기적으로 절감해줍니다.

09 명예의 전당, 우수협력기관 지정

우수교육기관은 'TOSEL 우수 협력 기관'에 지정되고, 각 시/도별, 최고득점자를 명예의 전당에 등재합니다.

Evaluation ——————— 평가

평가의 기본원칙

TOSEL은 PBT(Paper Based Test)를 통하여 간접평가와 직접평가를 모두 시행합니다.

TOSEL은 언어의 네 가지 요소인 **읽기, 듣기, 말하기, 쓰기 영역을 모두 평가합니다.**

문자언어   음성언어

읽기능력 + 듣기능력
쓰기능력   말하기능력

↓

대한민국 대표 영어능력 인증 시험제도

TOSEL®

Reading 읽기	모든 레벨의 읽기 영역은 직접 평가 방식으로 측정합니다.
Listening 듣기	모든 레벨의 듣기 영역은 직접 평가 방식으로 측정합니다.
Writing 쓰기	모든 레벨의 쓰기 영역은 간접 평가 방식으로 측정합니다.
Speaking 말하기	모든 레벨의 말하기 영역은 간접 평가 방식으로 측정합니다.

TOSEL은 연령별 인지단계를 고려하여 **아래와 같이 7단계로 나누어 평가합니다.**

1 단계		TOSEL® COCOON	5~7세의 미취학 아동
2 단계		TOSEL® Pre-STARTER	초등학교 1~2학년
3 단계		TOSEL® STARTER	초등학교 3~4학년
4 단계		TOSEL® BASIC	초등학교 5~6학년
5 단계		TOSEL® JUNIOR	중학생
6 단계		TOSEL® HIGH JUNIOR	고등학생
7 단계		TOSEL® ADVANCED	대학생 및 성인

Grade Report

개인 AI 정밀진단 성적표

십 수년간 전국단위 정기시험으로 축적된 빅데이터를 교육공학적으로 분석 · 활용하여 산출한 개인별 성적자료

정확한 영어능력진단 / 섹션별 · 파트별 영어능력 및 균형 진단 / 명예의 전당 등재 여부 / 온라인 최적화된 개인별 상세 성적자료를 위한 QR코드 / 응시지역, 동일학년, 전국에서의 학생의 위치

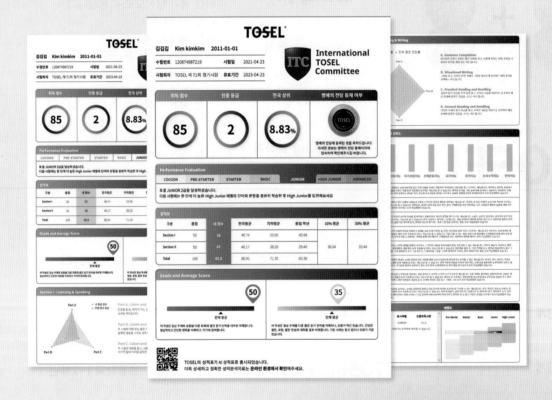

단체 및 기관 응시자 AI 통계 분석 자료

십 수년간 전국단위 정기시험으로 **축적된 빅데이터를
교육공학적으로 분석 · 활용**하여 산출한 응시자 통계 분석 자료

- 단체 내 레벨별 평균성적추이, LR평균 점수, 표준편차 파악
- 타 지역 내 다른 단체와의 점수 종합 비교 / 단체 내 레벨별
  학생분포 파악
- 동일 지역 내 다른 단체 레벨별 응시자의 평균 나이 비교
- 동일 지역 내 다른 단체 명예의 전당 등재 인원 수 비교
- 동일 지역 내 다른 단체 최고점자의 최고 점수 비교
- 동일 지역 내 다른 응시자들의 수 비교

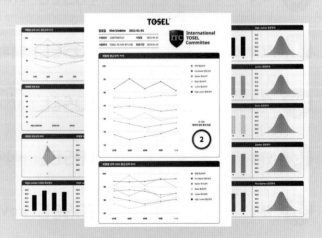

'토셀 명예의 전당' 등재

특별시, 광역시, 도 별 **1등 선발**
(**7**개시 9개도 **1등 선발**)

*홈페이지 로그인 - 시험결과 - 명예의 전당에서
 해당자 등재 증명서 출력 가능

'학업성취기록부'에 토셀 인증등급 기재

개인별 **'학업성취기록부'** 평생 발급
진학과 취업을 대비한 **필수 스펙관리**

인증서

대한민국 초,중,고등학생의 영어숙달능력 평가 결과 공식인증

고려대학교 인증획득 (2010. 03)   팬코리아영어교육학회 인증획득 (2009. 10)   한국응용언어학회 인증획득 (2009. 11)

한국외국어교육학회 인증획득 (2009. 12)   한국음성학회 인증획득 (2009. 12)

Listening Series

TOSEL 시험을 기준으로 빈출 지표를 활용한 문장 선정 및 예문과 문제 구성

TOSEL 시험 활용

- 실제 TOSEL 시험에 출제된 빈출 문항을 기준으로 단계별 학습을 위한 문장 선정

- 실제 TOSEL 시험에 활용된 문장을 사용하여 예문과 문제를 구성

- 듣기 학습 이외에 TOSEL 기출 문제 풀이를 통해서 TOSEL 및 실전 영어 시험 대비 학습

세분화된 레벨링

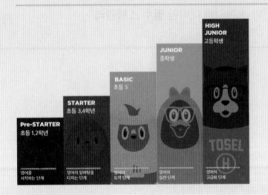

20년 간 대한민국 영어 평가 기관으로서

연간 4회 전국적으로 실시되는 정기시험에서

축적된 성적 데이터를 기반으로

정확하고 세분화된 레벨링을 통한

영어 학습 콘텐츠 개발

언어의 4대 영역 균형 학습 + 평가

1. **TOSEL 평가**: 학생의 영어 능력을 정확하게 평가

2. **결과 분석 및 진단**: 시험 점수와 결과를 분석하여 학생의 강점, 취약점, 학습자 특성 등을 객관적으로 진단

3. **학습 방향 제시**: 객관적 진단 데이터를 기반으로 학습자 특성에 맞는 학습 방향 제시 및 목표 설정

4. **학습**: 제시된 방향과 목표에 따라 학생에게 적합한 듣기 학습법 소개 및 영어의 체계와 구조 이해

5. **학습 목표 달성**: 학습 후 다시 평가를 통해 목표 달성 여부 확인 및 성장을 위한 다음 학습 목표 설정

Listening Series —————— Level

TOSEL의 Listening Series는 레벨에 맞게 단계적으로
영어 듣기를 학습할 수 있도록 구성되어 있습니다.

| **Pre-Starter** | **Starter** | **Basic** | **Junior** | **High Junior** |

■ 그림을 활용하여 어휘에 대한 이해도 향상

■ 다양한 활동을 통해 듣기 반복 학습 유도

■ TOSEL 기출 문제 연습을 통한 실전 대비

■ TOSEL 기출의 빈도수를 활용한 문장 선정으로 효율적 학습

■ 실제 TOSEL 지문의 예문을 활용한 실용적 학습 제공

■ TOSEL 기출 문제 연습을 통한 실전 대비

최신 수능 출제

어휘를 포함하여

수능 대비 가능

1시간 학습 Guideline

01
💡 Unit Intro
2분

02
📖 Before Practice
5분

■ 초등 교육과정에서 익혀야 하는 문장 패턴과 단어를
중심으로 단원의 학습내용에 대해 미리 생각해보기

■ 헷갈리는 발음에 대해 알아보고 예시 단어를 통해
발음 연습

■ 다양한 영어 표현을 듣고 따라해보면서 학습하기

05
✏️ Part B
10분

06
📖 Part C & Part D
10분

■ 대화를 듣고 빈칸에 알맞은 말을 쓴 다음, 문제에
맞는 답 고르기

■ 대화를 듣고 빈칸에 알맞은 말 쓰기

■ 다음으로 올 가장 적절한 응답 고르기

03
Practice

8분

■ 단어를 듣고 순서대로 철자에 알맞게 쓰기

■ 대화를 듣고 빈칸에 알맞은 단어 및 구 쓰기

04
Part A

10분

■ 대화를 듣고 빈칸에 알맞은 말을 쓴 다음, 문제에
맞는 답 고르기

07
Unit Review

5분

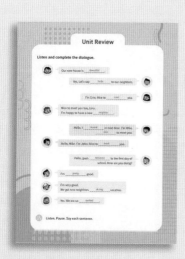

■ 빈칸을 채우는 형태로 구성하여 수업 시간 후
복습에 용이하게 구성

■ 배운 문장 패턴 및 단어를 활용하여 직접 써보는 시간

08
TOSEL 실전문제

10분

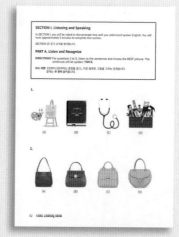

■ 실제 TOSEL 기출 문제를 통한 실전 대비 학습

■ 실제 시험 시간과 유사하게 풀이할 수 있도록 지도하기

■ 틀린 문제에 대해서는 해당 단원에서 복습하도록 지도하기

CHAPTER 01

Unit 01

인사 / 자기소개

Our new house is beautiful.

Yes, let's say hello to our neighbors.

I'm Lina. Nice to meet you.

Nice to meet you too, Lina.
I'm happy to have a new neighbor.

Hello, I moved in next door. I'm Mike.
Nice to meet you.

Hello, Mike. I'm John. Glad to meet you.

Hello, guys. Welcome to the first day
of school. How are you doing?

I'm pretty good.

I'm very good.
We got new neighbors during vacation.

Yes. We are so excited.

once	한 번	**year**	년, 해	**daily**	매일
twice	두 번	**routine**	일상	**weekly**	매주
forget	잊어버리다	**tomorrow**	내일	**yearly**	매년
week	주	**exercise**	운동하다	**next**	다음
month	달	**buy**	사다	**soon**	곧

Before Practice

Track 1-1-2

 토셀쌤의 Sound Tip

- 어려운 발음

introduce

u

[유]와 비슷하지만 더 긴 소리

student

June

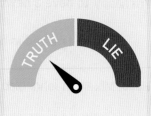
truth

flu

introduce

Expressions. Listen and learn the expressions.

glad to~
~해서 기쁘다

introduce oneself
자기소개 하다

get together
모이다

move in
이사하다

 **Practice**

Step 1. Listen to the words and write.

❶

❻

❷

❼

❸

❽

❹

❾

❺

❿

Step 2. Listen to the dialogue and fill in the blanks.

❶ B :   are you   ?

G : I'm   pretty   , thank you!   you?

❷ G : Let me   . I'm a   student. My   is art.

B : Can't believe it! I'm   art,   .

Let's   often!

Step 3. Complete the dialogue.

❶ B : What grade are you in?

G :

❷ B :   I moved in next door.

G : Nice to meet you. I'm Joanna. You can call me Jo.

Listen to the sentences and choose the best picture.

1.

> **G**: Jack is _____ hello to his new _____ .

(A)   (B)   (C)   (D)

2.

> **B**: My _____ is _____ .

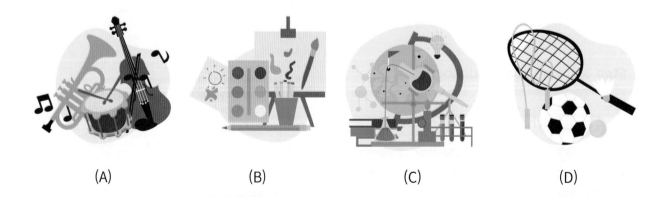

(A)   (B)   (C)   (D)

Part B. **Listen and Respond**

Track 1-1-5

 Listen to the sentences and choose the best response.

1.

B: **are you in?**

G: _____ .

(A) I am a   .

(B) I   Chicago.

(C) I   dogs.

(D) I am in the   .

2.

B: **Our new**   **in yesterday.**

G: _____ .

(A) You   great.

(B) They   home.

(C) I   at a school.

(D)   say hello to them.

3.

B: **are you**   **today?**

G: _____ .

(A)   good!

(B) See you   .

(C)   a nice day.

(D) Nice to   you.

Listen to the short talks or conversations and choose the best answer.

1.

> **B**: That box looks _____. Do you _____ help?
>
> **G**: Thank you, I just _____ today.

What is the girl doing?

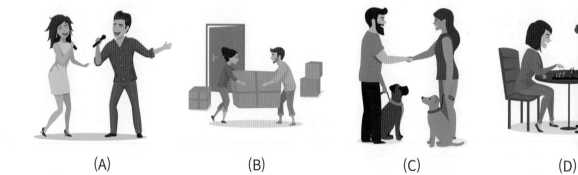

(A)   (B)   (C)   (D)

2.

> **B**: My _____ is _____. What's yours?
>
> **G**: I'm _____ mathematics.

What is the boy studying?

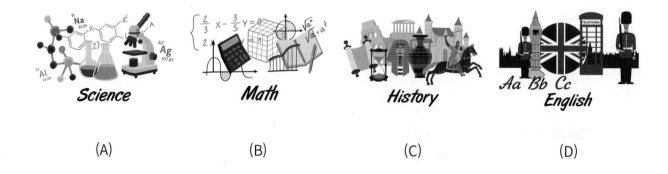

Science   Math   History   English

(A)   (B)   (C)   (D)

Part D. Listen and Speak

Track 1-1-7

 Listen to the conversations and choose the best response.

1.

> **W**: Good morning, class! We _____ a new _____ today.
>
> **B**: Hello, _____ . Pleased to meet you.
>
> **W**: Can you _____ _____ more about _____ ?

What's next?

(A) Yes, I am a student.

(B) My name is Minho.

(C) Yes, I'm fine, thank you.

(D) No thanks. I am very full.

2.

> **B**: Hello! _____ to Logan _____ School.
>
> **G**: Thank you! This is my _____ _____ of school.
>
> **B**: That's right. _____ are you _____ ?

What's next?

(A) No, I'm not.

(B) Yes, you are.

(C) I am so excited.

(D) It's raining outside.

Unit Review

Listen and complete the dialogue. ▶ Track 1-1-8

 Our new house is _____.

Yes, Let's say _____ to our neighbors.

I'm Lina. Nice to _____ you.

 Nice to meet you too, Lina.
I'm happy to have a new _____.

Hello, I _____ in next door. I'm Mike.
_____ to meet you.

 Hello, Mike. I'm John. Nice to _____ you.

Hello, guys. _____ to the first day of
school. How are you doing?

 I'm _____ good.

 I'm very good.
We got new neighbors _____ vacation.

 Yes. We are so _____.

 Listen. Pause. Say each sentence.

Unit 02

소개

 Let me introduce my family.
I have a lovely mom,
a strong dad and a cute little sister.

On the weekends, we go for a picnic.
We always have fun together.

You have a great family!

 We also go camping during the summer.
My dad plays the guitar and we sing together.

 I love my parents and my sister.

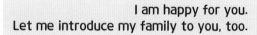

I am happy for you.
Let me introduce my family to you, too.

introduce	소개하다	**enjoy**	즐기다	**picnic**	소풍
little	작은	**parents**	부모	**weekend**	주말
also	또한	**summer**	여름	**share**	감정, 생각 등을 공유하다
favorite	가장 좋아하는	**fairy tale**	동화	**bank**	은행
bring	가져오다 (bring-brought-brought)	**younger**	더 어린	**friendly**	친절한, 다정한

Before Practice

▶ Track 1-2-2

 토셀쌤의 Sound Tip

• 어려운 발음

fai_r_y tale

ir

단어 중간이나 단어의 제일 끝에
위치했을 때 [어-]로 발음한다.

girl

bird

skirt

airport

 fairy tale

Expressions. Listen and learn the expressions.

enjoy reading
읽는 것을 즐기다

introduce oneself
자기소개 하다

talk about
~에 대해 이야기하다

work in
~에서 일하다

Practice

Step 1. Listen to the words and write.

❶ ⬜

❷ ⬜

❸ ⬜

❹ ⬜

❺ ⬜

❻ ⬜

❼ ⬜

❽ ⬜

❾ ⬜

❿ ⬜

Step 2. Listen to the dialogue and fill in the blanks.

❶ M: Everyone, we have a new student. Could you ⬜ yourself?

G: Hi, my name is Emily. I ⬜ reading ⬜ stories.

❷ G: John, could you ⬜ your favorite sport?

B: I enjoy ⬜ soccer. So, let me talk about soccer.

Step 3. Complete the dialogue.

❶ W: Brad, This is Julia, my younger sister. ⬜ .

M: Hello, Julia. I'm glad to meet you.

❷ G: ⬜ . Her name is Molly.

B: Oh, my dog is friendly with cats. Rocky, let's say hello to Molly.

 Track 1-2-4

 Listen to the sentences and choose the best picture.

1.

B: My father   in an Italian   .

(A)

(B)

(C)

(D)

2.

G: My grandmother   us   in the evening.

(A)

(B)

(C)

(D)

Part B. **Listen and Respond**

 Track 1-2-5

Listen to the sentences and choose the best response.

1.

> **B**: I would like to _____ a story about my _____ .
> **G**: _____ .

(A) I can't _____ to hear it.
(B) It _____ last week.
(C) The story was very _____ .
(D) _____ would you like to read?

2.

> **B**: _____ type of _____ do you like most?
> **G**: _____ .

(A) I _____ a lot of fruit.
(B) He doesn't like _____ food.
(C) I _____ eating in Indian restaurants.
(D) He _____ kimbap, a Korean food.

3.

> **B**: Could you _____ your _____ music?
> **G**: _____ .

(A) The sound is too _____ .
(B) I _____ in a music company.
(C) I enjoy _____ to pop music.
(D) No, I went to the concert by _____ .

 Listen to the short talks or conversations and choose the best answer.

1.

B: Olivia, ⬚ is Aiden, ⬚ friend from ⬚ school.

G: It's a ⬚ to ⬚ you.

What is the boy's high school friend's name?

HELLO MY NAME IS **Olivia**	HELLO MY NAME IS **Aiden**	HELLO MY NAME IS **Peter**	HELLO MY NAME IS **Harvey**
(A)	(B)	(C)	(D)

2.

G: I want to ⬚ my ⬚ doll to you.

B: She has blue ⬚ and ⬚ hair!

What is the girl's favorite doll?

| (A) | (B) | (C) | (D) |

Part D. **Listen and Speak**

Track 1-2-7

 Listen to the conversations and choose the best response.

1.

M: Hello! My _____ is Alex Litterman, the new _____.

W: Good morning. I'm Mia Webb. _____ to _____ you.

M: Mia, _____ _____ Mr. Anderson, your coworker.

What's next?

(A) This is my father.

(B) How did you do it?

(C) Where did you go?

(D) I'm glad to meet you.

2.

B: Yuna, _____ _____ hello to my cat, Clover.

G: Oh, she is _____ _____ !

B: Well, actually, _____ cat is a _____.

What's next?

(A) Who is she?

(B) Are you okay?

(C) Really? I'm sorry.

(D) No, I don't have any.

Unit Review

Listen and complete the dialogue.

▶ Track 1-2-8

 Let me _____ my family.
I have a _____ mom, a _____
dad and a cute little sister.

 On the _____ we go for a picnic.
We always have fun _____.

You have a _____ family!

 We also go _____ during the _____.
My dad plays the _____ and we sing together.

 I _____ my parents and my sister.

I am happy for you.
Let me _____ my _____ to you, too.

 Listen. Pause. Say each sentence.

Unit 03

묘사

 I brought a picture of my bedroom to share with you.

I brought mine too.
My bedroom is full of fun toys.
You will love them.

 This is my bedroom.
I have a rocking horse beside my small desk.

Wow, I want to try the rocking horse!

Ta-da! What do you think of my bedroom?
I have lots of bricks to play with.

 I want to make a castle too.

rocking horse	흔들 목마	**picture**	사진	**full**	가득한
beside	옆에	**try**	시도해 보다	**brick**	벽돌
castle	성	**bedroom**	침실	**describe**	묘사하다
tray	쟁반	**behind**	뒤에	**beneath**	아래에, 밑에
grass	풀, 잔디	**stand**	서 있다	**toy**	장난감

Before Practice

Track 1-3-2

토셀쌤의 Sound Tip

• 어려운 발음

beneath

th

teeth

mouth

earth

bath

단어가 <u>th</u>로 끝나면
<u>[-뜨, -ㅅ뜨]</u>로 발음한다.

beneath

Expressions. Listen and learn the expressions.

side by side
나란히

in front of
~앞에

share with
~와 나누다

lie down
눕다

Practice

Step 1. Listen to the words and write.

❶

❻

❷

❼

❸

❽

❹

❾

❺

❿

Step 2. Listen to the dialogue and fill in the blanks.

❶ **B**: Can you _____ the cup on the table?

G: There is a tray _____ the cup.

❷ **B**: Is Ben _____ _____ you?

G: No, Ben is _____ John.

Step 3. Complete the dialogue.

❶ **G**: Where are the children in the classroom?

B: _____

❷ **G**: What is Ben doing with his pet, Charlie, at the park?

B: _____

Listen to the sentences and choose the best picture.

1.

B: The children are _____ their _____ .

(A)

(B)

(C)

(D)

2.

G: I like the _____ blanket and the _____ in my bedroom.

(A)

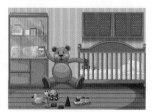

(B)

(C)

(D)

Part B. **Listen and Respond**

 Listen to the sentences and choose the best response.

1.

> **B**:   are they   in the room?
>
> **G**: _____.

(A) It is   the table.

(B) He is   a letter.

(C) She is   an apple.

(D) They are   side by side.

2.

> **B**: There is a watch   the pencil case.
>
> **G**: _____.

(A) That is   .

(B) Yes, there   .

(C) I'm   TV.

(D) It's in your   .

3.

> **B**: I see a very   table   the bed.
>
> **G**: _____.

(A) No,   .

(B)   you see them?

(C) I like your ncw   .

(D) I   it yesterday.

 Listen to the short talks or conversations and choose the best answer.

1.

> **G**: A cat ⬜⬜⬜ a dog ⬜⬜⬜ ⬜⬜⬜ down together.
>
> **B**: I ⬜⬜⬜ ! Who is the ⬜⬜⬜ ?

What are the cat and dog doing?

(A)　　　　　　(B)　　　　　　(C)　　　　　　(D)

2.

> **G**: ⬜⬜⬜ you ⬜⬜⬜ the room to ⬜⬜⬜ ?
>
> **B**: There ⬜⬜⬜ lots of ⬜⬜⬜ to ⬜⬜⬜ .

What does the room look like?

(A)　　　　　　(B)　　　　　　(C)　　　　　　(D)

Part D. **Listen and Speak**

Track 1-3-7

 Listen to the conversations and choose the best response.

1.

> **M**: We are ⬚ ⬚ for the meeting.
> **W**: Let's ⬚ and ⬚ the bus.
> **M**: ⬚ ⬚ the bus?

What's next?

(A) Where are they?

(B) He is in the hospital.

(C) The bus is going to the airport.

(D) It's standing in front of the gate.

2.

> **B**: Hello, Jena. ⬚ are you ⬚ ?
> **G**: I ⬚ my family picture to ⬚ you.
> **B**: Let me see. ⬚ are you in this ⬚ ?

What's next?

(A) He jumped into the water.

(B) There's someone behind you.

(C) I am sitting beside my mother.

(D) Don't put your feet on the table.

Unit Review

Listen and complete the dialogue.

 Track 1-3-8

 I _____ a picture of my bedroom to share with you.

I brought mine too. My _____ is full of fun toys. You will _____ them.

 This is my bedroom. I have a _____ horse _____ my small desk.

Wow, I _____ to try the rocking horse!

 Ta-da! What do you _____ of my bedroom? I have lots of _____ to play _____.

I want to make a _____ too.

 Listen. Pause. Say each sentence.

TOSEL 실전문제 ❶

QR코드를 인식시키면
음원이 재생됩니다

1.

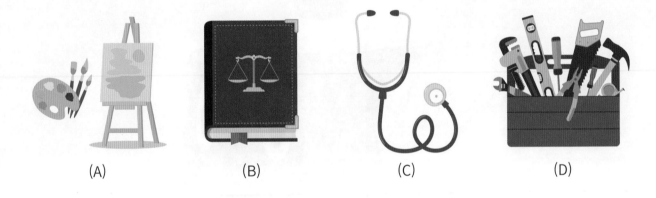

(A)　　　　　(B)　　　　　(C)　　　　　(D)

2.

(A)　　　　　(B)　　　　　(C)　　　　　(D)

3.

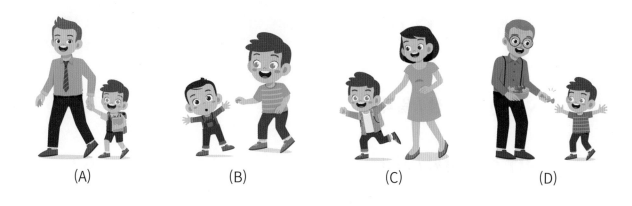

(A)   (B)   (C)   (D)

4.

(A)   (B)   (C)   (D)

5.

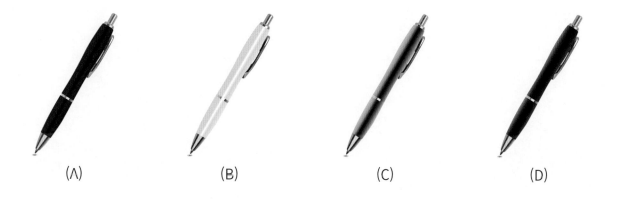

(A)   (B)   (C)   (D)

CHAPTER 02

Unit 01

일상 / 일과

Hello, what are you doing so early in the morning?

I always go jogging in the mornings.
My day normally starts at 7 AM.

I usually run from Monday to Friday.
During weekends, I never get up before 9 AM.

Then, how do you spend the weekends?

I spend my weekends reading books
and chatting with my friends. What about you?

On Sundays, I like going to the movies with
Emma in downtown.

Emma? Isn't she your neighbor?
How often do you see her?

I see her once a week.
Let's get together this weekend and hang out.

Oh, really? I would love to.

early	이른, 빠른	**before**	~전에, 앞에	**free time**	자유 시간
jog	조깅하다	**chat**	수다를 떨다, 채팅하다	**sometimes**	때때로, 가끔
normally	보통, 정상적으로	**once a week**	일주일에 한 번	**downtown**	번화가
usually	부통, 대개	**around**	약, 쯤, 주위에	**often**	자주, 흔히
never	결코 ~않다	**every**	모든, 매~	**twice**	두 번, 두 배로

Before Practice

Track 2-1-2

토셀쌤의 Sound Tip

• 어려운 발음

usu**a**lly

a

[a]에 강세가 오지 않을 때
[어] 비슷한 소리로 발음한다.

around

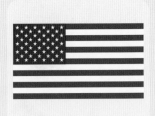
America

village

message

usually

Expressions. Listen and learn the expressions.

spend time ~ing
~하면서 시간을 보내다

drive ~ to ~
~로 운전해서 가다

hang out
~와 시간을 보내다

dress up
차려입다

 **Practice**

Step 1. Listen to the words and write.

❶

❷

❸

❹

❺

❻

❼

❽

❾

❿

Step 2. Listen to the dialogue and fill in the blanks.

❶ G: do you   get up?

　 B: 7 o'clock. I like to dress up   morning.

❷ G: Nicole,   do you   your   ?

　 B: I spend my free time   with my friends   the beach.

Step 3. Complete the dialogue.

❶ G: You are never late to school.

　 B: I take the subway. Sometimes, my parents drive me to school.

❷ B: You dance so well!

　 G: I dance once a week. I sing twice a week.

Basic 47

 Listen to the sentences and choose the best picture.

1.

G: Joe and I go ⬜⬜⬜ at the beach ⬜⬜⬜ weekend.

(A) (B) (C) (D)

2.

B: He ⬜⬜⬜ ⬜⬜⬜ the dishes after ⬜⬜⬜ .

(A) (B) (C) (D)

 Listen to the sentences and choose the best response.

1.

> M : What time does she _____ to _____ ?
>
> W : _____ .

(A) She is _____ her teeth.

(B) She _____ home at 8:40 AM.

(C) She gets up _____ 6 AM.

(D) She gets to work _____ 9 AM.

2.

> B : _____ he play video games at _____ ?
>
> G : _____ .

(A) I do it _____ day.

(B) He _____ plays it.

(C) No, he _____ do it.

(D) He is _____ a shower.

3.

> B : How _____ do you get _____ from her?
>
> G : _____ .

(A) Yes, a _____ .

(B) It's _____ .

(C) One _____ one.

(D) Twice a _____ .

 Listen to the short talks or conversations and choose the best answer.

1.

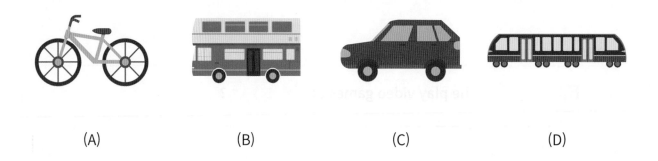

B: _____ do you _____ to school?

G: I usually _____ a _____.

How does the girl go to school?

(A)   (B)   (C)   (D)

2.

G: How _____ do you go to an _____?

B: My grandfather _____ takes me there _____ a _____.

Where does the boy go once a month?

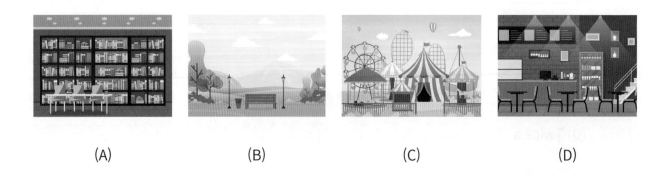

(A)   (B)   (C)   (D)

Part D. **Listen and Speak**

✏️ **Listen to the conversations and choose the best response.**

1.

> **B**: Hello, I _____ to _____ John. I'm his friend.
>
> **G**: Sorry, he's _____ home _____ now.
>
> **B**: Then, _____ can I _____ him?

What's next?

(A) He goes to bed around 9.

(B) He is crazy about basketball.

(C) He's always at the gym at this time.

(D) He had dinner with his family at 7.

2.

> **B**: How do you _____ the Sunday _____ ?
>
> **G**: I _____ spend time _____ books.
>
> **B**: Do you read books _____ _____ ?

What's next?

(A) No, at a cafe.

(B) Yes, at the party.

(C) No, it was boring.

(D) Every Sunday.

Unit Review

Listen and complete the dialogue.

 Hello, what are you doing in this _____ morning?

 I always go _____ in the mornings.
My day _____ starts at 7 AM.

I usually run from _____ to _____.
During weekends, I _____ get up before 9 AM.

 Then, how do you _____ the weekends?

I spend my weekends _____ books and
_____ with my friends. What about you?

 On Sundays, I like _____ to the _____ with
Emma in downtown.

 Emma? Isn't she your neighbor?
_____ _____ do you see her?

 I see her _____ a week.
Let's get together this weekend and _____ _____.

Oh, really? I would _____ to.

 Listen. Pause. Say each sentence.

Unit 02

날씨 / 시간

 What's the weather like today?

 It's really sunny today.
Do you want to ride the bicycle with me today?

 Sounds great! What time should we meet?

 Let's meet at 4 PM.

 This is exciting!

 Yes. We should ride our bicycles more often!

sunny	화창한	**PM**	오후	**ride**	타고 달리다
forget	잊어버리다	**take**	(교통수단 등을) 타다, (얼마의 시간이) 걸리다	**skill**	기량, 기술
half	절반	**month**	달, 월	**should**	~해야 한다
around	약	**season**	계절	**windy**	바람이 많이 부는
AM	오전	**because**	~때문에	**favorite**	가장 좋아하는

토셀쌤의 Sound Tip

• 어려운 발음

half

L

[D, F, K, M] 소리 앞의 L은
발음하지 않는다.

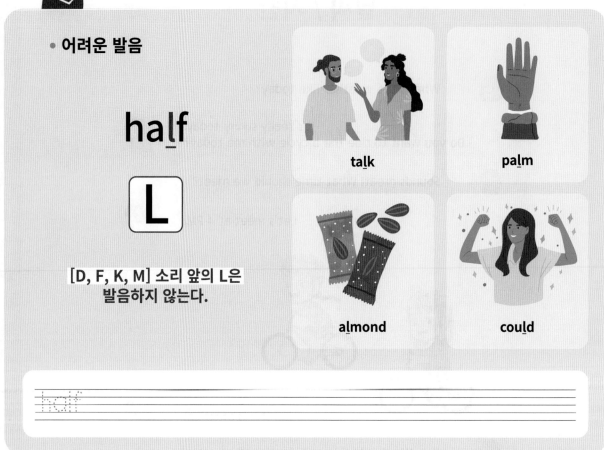

talk

palm

almond

could

half

Expressions. Listen and learn the expressions.

take the bus
버스를 타다

put on
~를 입다/쓰다

play in the snow
눈에서 놀다

pick up
(습관/재주 등을) 익히다

 **Practice**

 Track 2-2-3

Step 1. Listen to the words and write.

❶

❷

❸

❹

❺

❻

❼

❽

❾

❿

Step 2. Listen to the dialogue and fill in the blanks.

❶ **G**: What's the _____ like _____ ?

B: It's going to be really _____ . Don't _____ to put on a _____ .

❷ **G**: What _____ will you _____ to my _____ ?

B: _____ _____ AM. I am _____ the _____ now.

Step 3. Complete the dialogue.

❶ **B**: What is your favorite season?

G:

❷ **B**:

G: It took one and a half months.

Listen to the sentences and choose the best picture.

1.

B: You should always wear _____ even on _____ days.

(A)

(B)

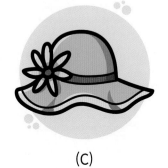

(C)

(D)

2.

G: It _____ two _____ by plane from London to Madrid.

(A)

(B)

(C)

(D)

 Listen to the sentences and choose the best response.

1.

B: What's the _____ _____ in Russia?

G: _____.

(A) It's _____ .

(B) It's _____ past ten.

(C) It's freezing _____ .

(D) There was a _____ .

2.

B: _____ time is it? We're going to be _____ !

G: _____.

(A) Sure, we _____ .

(B) It's _____ 14th.

(C) It's _____ 5 o'clock.

(D) There is a _____ coming.

3.

M: Welcome to our hotel. _____ will you stay?

W: _____.

(A) Not very _____ .

(B) For about five _____ .

(C) At my friend's _____ .

(D) It _____ a long time to go there.

 Listen to the short talks or conversations and choose the best answer.

1.

G: _____ are you wearing a _____?

B: The TV says _____ is going to _____ soon.

What is the boy wearing?

(A)   (B)   (C)   (D)

2.

B: What is your _____ _____?

G: It's _____ because I can sit _____ a fireplace with a book.

Why does the girl like winter?

(A)   (B)   (C)   (D)

Part D. **Listen and Speak**

Track 2-2-7

 Listen to the conversations and choose the best response.

1.

> **B:**   do I   ? Isn't it nice?
>
> **G:** Just a sweater? It will   this   .
>
> **B:** What   I   then?

What's next?

   (A) It is not so hot today.

   (B) We should go skating.

   (C) My favorite season is spring.

   (D) You should put on a jacket.

2.

> **B:** You   happy. What's   ?
>
> **G:** I just   this book.
>
> **B:** How long   it   ?

What's next?

   (A) I am so excited.

   (B) Every ten minutes.

   (C) It took me three days.

   (D) It's about two kilometers from here.

Unit Review

Listen and complete the dialogue. ▶ Track 2-2-8

 What's the _____ like today?

 It's really _____ today. Do you want to _____ the _____ with me today?

 Sounds great! _____ _____ will you meet me?

 Let's meet _____ 4 PM.

 This is _____!

 Yes. We _____ ride the bicycle more _____!

🗣 Listen. Pause. Say each sentence.

Unit 03

상태 / 건강

This summer is way too hot.

Yeah, I am exhausted.

I want to spend time at the beach.
I love swimming. What about you, Sarah?

I am tired from the heat.
I want to have ice cream instead.

I have an idea! Come with me.

Let's take a rest while enjoying our ice cream!

It's perfect! I feel better now.

exhausted	지친	**rest**	휴식	**excellent**	훌륭한
spend	(시간을) 보내다	**instead**	대신에	**practice**	연습하다
until	~까지	**stay**	(상태를) 유지하다	**calm**	차분한, 침착한
no way	말도 안돼!	**tired**	피곤한	**give back**	돌려주다
sleepy	졸리운, 졸음이 오는	**annoyed**	짜증이 난	**exam**	시험

Before Practice

(►) Track 2-3-2

 토셀쌤의 Sound Tip

- 어려운 발음

e<u>x</u>am

X

[X : 위치에 따라 소리가 달라진다]

① x가 맨 끝에 나오면 [ㅋ-ㅅ]
② ex뒤에 모음이 오면 [ㄱ-ㅈ]
③ ex뒤에 자음이 오면 [ㅋ-ㅆ]

rela<u>x</u>

e<u>x</u>hausted

e<u>x</u>cellent

e<u>x</u>tra

Expressions. Listen and learn the expressions.

**get some rest
= take a rest**
쉬다

give money back
돈을 돌려주다

take an exam
시험을 보다

tired from
~로 인해 피곤하다

 **Practice**

Step 1. Listen to the words and write.

❶
❻

❷
❼

❸
❽

❹
❾

❺
❿

Step 2. Listen to the dialogue and fill in the blanks.

❶ B: I   for 5 hours. I'm   .

G: now? No way. You should   some   .

❷ B: You are so   . Stay   .

G: How can I stay   ? He didn't   my money   .

Step 3. Complete the dialogue.

❶ W:

M: I made cookies for my students yesterday.

❷ M: You have studied for a long time today. Go to sleep.

G: Dad,

 Listen to the sentences and choose the best picture.

1.

M : I'm _____ from work, but I'm not _____ .

(A)   (B)   (C)   (D)

2.

B : The teacher was _____ _____ some _____ .

(A)   (B)   (C)   (D)

 Listen to the sentences and choose the best response.

1.

> **B**: Can you   the   please?
>
> **G**: _____.

(A) Yes, a   .
(B) No, it is   .
(C) Are you   ?
(D) Are you going   ?

2.

> **B**: Diane   a   in front of her class.
>
> **G**: _____.

(A) Please be   .
(B) She is so   !
(C) The exam was   .
(D) The film wasn't very   .

3.

> **B**: I don't   today.
>
> **G**: _____.

(A)   is it going?
(B)   were you?
(C) I studied until   .
(D) You   see a doctor.

 Listen to the short talks or conversations and choose the best answer.

1.

B: I want to _____ more _____ in the _____ .
G: No, you should _____ _____ _____ now.

What does the boy want to do?

(A)   (B)   (C)   (D)

2.

B: Let's go _____ this _____ .
G: Sorry, climbing the _____ makes _____ feel _____ .

Why doesn't the girl go hiking?

(A)   (B)   (C)   (D)

 Listen to the conversations and choose the best response.

1.

> B: is the   with you?
>
> G: I'm   with my mom.
>
> B: You know, she   angry for a long time.

What's next?

    (A) Yes, I am nervous.

    (B) He will stay for a week.

    (C) She works hard but I don't.

    (D) Yes, I should say sorry to her.

2.

> M: is your   .
>
> W: Thank you.   is it?
>
> M: 10 dollars. You may   after taking this.

What's next?

    (A) That's a good idea.

    (B) The room is way too hot.

    (C) Alright, I'll remember that.

    (D) It's perfect! You look great.

Unit Review

Listen and complete the dialogue.

▶ Track 2-3-8

 This _____ is way too hot.

Yeah, I am _____.

I want to _____ _____ at the beach.
I love _____. What about you, Sarah?

 I am _____ from the _____.
I want to have _____ instead.

I have an _____! Come with me.

Let's take a _____ while _____ our ice cream!

 It's perfect! I feel _____ now.

 Listen. Pause. Say each sentence.

TOSEL 실전문제 ②

QR코드를 인식시키면
음원이 재생됩니다

1.

(A)　　　　　　(B)　　　　　　(C)　　　　　　(D)

2.

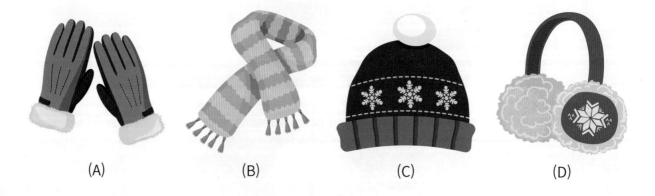

(A)　　　　　　(B)　　　　　　(C)　　　　　　(D)

3.

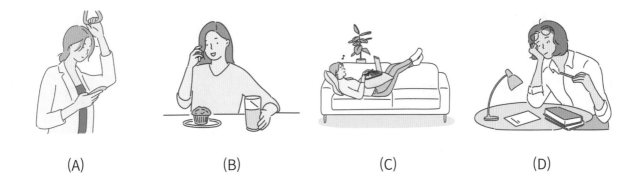

(A)   (B)   (C)   (D)

4.

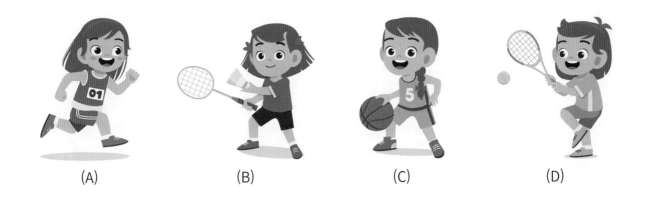

(A)   (B)   (C)   (D)

5.

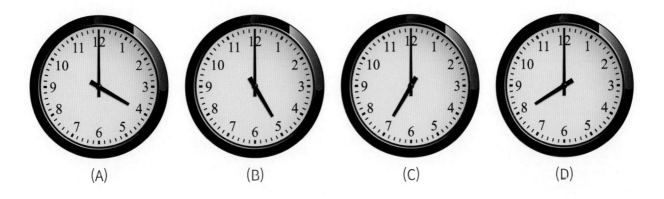

(A)   (B)   (C)   (D)

CHAPTER 03

Unit 01

기쁨 / 기대

Track 3-1-1

 Class, we will be going on a field trip to an amusement park next week.

Mrs. Smith, I have an idea. It would be amazing if we could ride a roller coaster.

I am so excited.

I got an idea too! Can we take class photos at the end?

 That is a wonderful idea, Jane!

I am so thrilled, I just can't wait. Oh, I should get some new clothes for the pictures.

amusement park 놀이공원	**thrilled** 신이 난	**jump** 점프, 점프하다
idea 아이디어	**leave** 남기다 (leave-left-left)	**joy** 기쁨, 즐거움
amazing 멋진, 훌륭한	**laptop** 노트북 컴퓨터	**another** 또 하나의, 다른
roller coaster 롤러코스터	**serious** 진지한	**ride** 타다
end 끝, 끝나다	**classmate** 반 친구	**autograph** (유명인의) 사인

UNIT 1 기쁨 / 기대

 Before Practice

🔊 토셀쌤의 Sound Tip

Track 3-1-2

- 어려운 발음

thri_ll_ed

쌍자음
(DD, FF, MM, NN, LL, RR, SS…)

영어 쌍자음을 발음할 때는 대표음 하나만 발음한다.

cli_ff_

di_nn_er

su_mm_er

ho_rr_or

Expressions. Listen and learn the expressions.

ride a roller coaster
롤러코스터를 타다

travel to (place)
~로 여행하다

make someone's day
~덕분에 기분이 좋아지다

jump for joy
기뻐서 날뛰다

 **Practice**

Track 3-1-3

Step 1. Listen to the words and write.

❶

❷

❸

❹

❺

❻

❼

❽

❾

❿

Step 2. Listen to the dialogue and fill in the blanks.

❶ G: I _____ _____ to see your new _____ !
   B: I'm _____ too. Only two months left.

❷ G: I will buy you a _____ laptop for your birthday.
   B: Are you serious? Thank you. You just made my day!

Step 3. Complete the dialogue.

❶ B: Did you hear about the plan this weekend?
   G: Yes, _____

❷ B: Our classmates jump for joy at the news.
   G: _____

 Listen to the sentences and choose the best picture.

1.

B: I'm ____ forward to ____ a new ____ salon.

(A)   (B)   (C)   (D)

2.

G: I was ____ that we could ____ ____ for real.

(A)   (B)   (C)   (D)

 Listen to the sentences and choose the best response.

1.

M: _____ your son like the new _____?

W: _____ .

(A) He _____ for joy.

(B) She _____ for an hour.

(C) I couldn't _____ laughing.

(D) He _____ a bus to school.

2.

B: Did you _____ that Jane _____ the gold medal?

G: _____ .

(A) I'm sorry to _____ that.

(B) I can't _____ to see the ending.

(C) Sorry, I am not in a good _____ .

(D) Yes, I was thrilled at the good _____ .

3.

B: I _____ a love _____ today.

G: _____ .

(A) What's the _____ ?

(B) I am sorry. I _____ it.

(C) Thank you for the _____ .

(D) That's _____ . I envy you.

 Listen to the short talks or conversations and choose the best answer.

1.

> **B**: This is your _____. You can _____ it to _____.
>
> **G**: Oh, it is a _____ _____. Thank you. I _____ this.

What was the present?

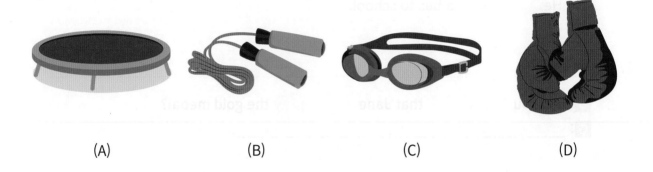

| (A) | (B) | (C) | (D) |

2.

> **B**: Isn't this your _____? I think you _____ it in the _____.
>
> **G**: Wow, you found my _____! You just _____ my day!

What did the boy find for the girl?

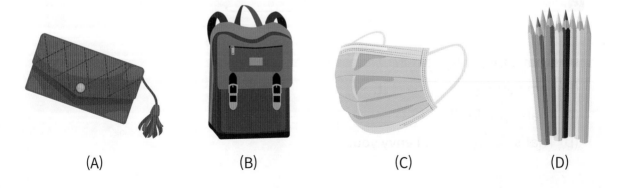

| (A) | (B) | (C) | (D) |

 Listen to the conversations and choose the best response.

1.

> **B:** _____ you hear the _____ news?
>
> **G:** No, not _____ . What is it _____ ?
>
> **B:** We _____ first _____ in the singing _____ !

What's next?

    (A) I am bad at singing.

    (B) You really think so?

    (C) That's not too bad.

    (D) I can't believe it's true!

2.

> **B:** _____ you going to the rock _____ tomorrow?
>
> **G:** I already _____ the _____ .
>
> **B:** You look very _____ . Will you get their _____ ?

What's next?

    (A) No, I don't like rock music.

    (B) Do you have a ticket to enter?

    (C) Of course. I can't wait to meet them.

    (D) Oh, dear. I am so happy to hear that.

UNIT 1 기본 / 기타

Unit Review

Listen and complete the dialogue.

 Class, we will be _____ on a field trip to an _____ park next week.

 Mrs. Smith, I have an idea. It _____ be amazing if we could ride a _____ _____.

 I am so _____.

 I got an _____ too! Can we _____ class photos at the end?

 That is a _____ idea Jane!

 I am so _____, I just _____ _____ for it. Oh, I _____ get some new clothes for the pictures.

 Listen. Pause. Say each sentence.

Unit 02

Track 3-2-1

소망 / 소원

 Mom, what do you hope to get for your birthday?

It's okay. There's nothing I wish for.

 What can I do for her? I have an idea!

 I hope that mom likes this cake.

 Happy birthday! I hope you have a wonderful day.

I also wish you a happy day. Love you!

wish	원하다, 바라다, 소망	**birthday**	생일	**get**	받다
hope	바라다, 희망하다	**share**	나누다, 공유하다	**wish list**	소원 목록
lottery	복권	**Christmas**	크리스마스	**laptop**	노트북
win	이기다	**final exam**	기말 시험	**roommate**	룸메이트
really	실제로, 정말로	**New Year's Day**	새해 첫날	**true**	사실인, 진짜의

Before Practice

 Track 3-2-2

 토셀쌤의 Sound Tip

• 어려운 발음

wish<u>ed</u>
hop<u>ed</u>

-ed → [t]

① 모양은 wished → 발음은 [wisht]로
한다는 것 주의!
② 모양은 hoped → 발음은 [hopt]로
한다는 것 주의!

finish<u>ed</u>

work<u>ed</u>

help<u>ed</u>

mix<u>ed</u>

Expressions. Listen and learn the expressions.

make a wish
소원을 빌다

come true
이루어지다

pass the exam
시험을 통과하다

win the lottery
복권에 당첨되다

Practice

Step 1. Listen to the words and write.

❶   ❻

❷   ❼

❸   ❽

❹   ❾

❺   ❿

Step 2. Listen to the dialogue and fill in the blanks.

❶ G: What do you   to   for   ?
    B: I   to get a   .

❷ G: Let's share our wish list. What   did you   ?
    B: I   for a   laptop. And it really came true!

Step 3. Complete the dialogue.

❶ B:
    G: I hope that we can. And I hope that you are my roommate next year.

❷ G: What did you wish for on New Year's Day?
    B:

 Listen to the sentences and choose the best picture.

1.

G : For my   , I hope I will get a   .

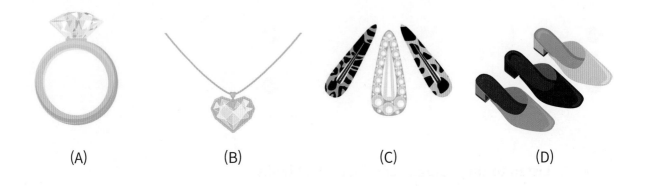

(A)   (B)   (C)   (D)

2.

B : Joan is hoping to become a   .

(A)   (B)   (C)   (D)

 Listen to the sentences and choose the best response.

1.

> B : He just made a _____ !
>
> G : _____.

(A) Wish me _____ !

(B) _____ did he wish for?

(C) When is your _____ ?

(D) What kind of _____ does he want?

2.

> B : What did the girl _____ _____ ?
>
> G : _____.

(A) _____ _____ about it.

(B) She wrote a _____ _____ .

(C) I hope _____ works out.

(D) She hoped the _____ would end soon.

3.

> B : Beth always wished that she could _____ _____ a big house.
>
> G : _____.

(A) Do you _____ it?

(B) _____ were you?

(C) Did it come _____ ?

(D) What is _____ ?

 Listen to the short talks or conversations and choose the best answer.

1.

> B : I _____ my suitcase. I think I left it in the _____ .
>
> G : Let's just hope someone _____ it and calls you.

What did the boy lose?

(A)   (B)   (C)   (D)

2.

> G : I wish to spend my vacation in _____ .
>
> B : I wish I could be there _____ _____ .

Where does the boy wish to go next year?

(A)   (B)   (C)   (D)

 Listen to the conversations and choose the best response.

1.

> **B**: I'm the ⬚⬚⬚⬚⬚ ⬚⬚⬚⬚⬚. Tell me your three ⬚⬚⬚⬚⬚.
>
> **G**: My ⬚⬚⬚⬚ wish is to go on a ⬚⬚⬚⬚ trip.
>
> **B**: Okay, what is your ⬚⬚⬚⬚ wish?

What's next?

(A) I didn't go to work today.

(B) I am going to do my homework.

(C) I will pay more attention in class.

(D) I wish I could speak English well.

2.

> **B**: It rained a lot ⬚⬚⬚⬚.
>
> **G**: I know! The ⬚⬚⬚⬚ stopped because of the ⬚⬚⬚⬚.
>
> **B**: I hope that the ⬚⬚⬚⬚ is good today.

What's next?

(A) Sure, it is.

(B) I hope so, too.

(C) Yes, of course.

(D) That's too bad.

Unit Review

Listen and complete the dialogue.

▶ Track 3-2-8

 Mom, what do you _____ to get for your _____?

 It's okay. There's nothing I _____ _____.

 What _____ I do for her? I have an idea!

 I hope that mom _____ this cake.

 _____ birthday! I _____ you have a wonderful day.

 I also _____ you a happy day. Love you!

 Listen. Pause. Say each sentence.

Unit 03

 Track 3-3-1

불만 / 슬픔

 Why are you crying John?

I fell down and broke my favorite truck.

 Don't be sad. I have a great idea!
Let's ask dad if he can fix your truck.

 Don't worry, John. Your truck can be fixed.

 I will fix it right away.
So, no more long face... okay?

Okay...

 Here you go, John. Good as new!

Yay! Thank you, dad!

fall	넘어지다	**break** (break-broke-broken)	부서지다	**fix**	고치다
problem	문제	**stain**	얼룩	**long face**	시무룩한 얼굴
right away	곧바로, 즉시	**fight**	싸움, 싸우다	**pasta**	파스타
salty	소금이 든, 짭짤한	**check**	확인하다	**well**	좋은, 건강한
hospital	병원	**bad**	나쁜, 미안한	**enough**	충분한

Before Practice

▶ Track 3-3-2

토셀쌤의 Sound Tip

- 어려운 발음

fi**gh**t

gh

light

sigh

① [ㄱ] **gh**ost : 단어 맨 앞에 올 때
② [ㅍ] enou**gh**: 단어 맨 끝에 올 때
③ [소리 안남] fi**gh**t : 단어 중간, [t] 앞에 올 때
④ [소리 안남] hi**gh** : [아이, 에이] 모음이 앞에 있을 때

Ghana

laugh**

Expressions. Listen and learn the expressions.

fight with ~
~랑 싸우다

check
~을 확인하다

get sleep
잠을 자다

fall down
넘어지다

 **Practice**

Step 1. Listen to the words and write.

1

2

3

4

5

6

7

8

9

10

Step 2. Listen to the dialogue and fill in the blanks.

1 **B**: Is there a　　　　　with your　　　　　?
　　G: Yes. I am　　　　　about the　　　　　on this　　　　　.

2 **B**: Why the　　　　　　　　　　?
　　G: I　　　　　with my　　　　　yesterday.

Step 3. Complete the dialogue.

1 **W**:
　　M: I am sorry. I'll check on it right away.

2 **G**:
　　B: That's too bad. You should get enough sleep.

Listen to the sentences and choose the best picture.

1.

G : He had a ⬚ with his ⬚ neighbor.

(A)

(B)

(C)

(D)

2.

B : I was feeling ⬚ because I ⬚ the math ⬚ .

(A)

(B)

(C)

(D)

 Listen to the sentences and choose the best response.

1.

> **B**: I don't ▢▢▢ ▢▢▢ today, so I can't meet you.
>
> **G**: _____.

(A) He is in the ▢▢▢ .

(B) I hope you ▢▢▢ soon.

(C) I can't thank you ▢▢▢ .

(D) ▢▢▢ are you going now?

2.

> **M**: Excuse me, my ▢▢▢ is not cooked ▢▢▢ .
>
> **W**: _____.

(A) I am going to ▢▢▢ with it.

(B) The food is cold and ▢▢▢ .

(C) I'm very sorry. I'll send it ▢▢▢ .

(D) It tastes good, but it's too ▢▢▢ .

3.

> **B**: Owen ▢▢▢ be ▢▢▢ again.
>
> **G**: _____.

(A) How are you ▢▢▢ ?

(B) You hurt my ▢▢▢ .

(C) I can't ▢▢▢ this anymore.

(D) I am in a good ▢▢▢ today.

 Listen to the short talks or conversations and choose the best answer.

1.

> **B**:   is   ?
>
> **G**: I am   angry! I   a fly in my   .

Why is the girl angry?

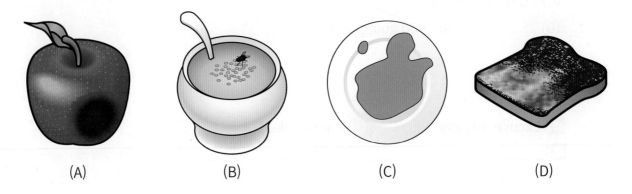

(A)	(B)	(C)	(D)

2.

> **G**: Is there a   your shoes?
>
> **B**: Yes, I   last week, but they're   big.

What is the boy's problem?

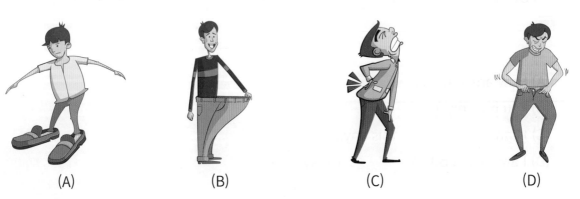

(A)	(B)	(C)	(D)

 Listen to the conversations and choose the best response.

1.

> M: _____ me, I'm _____ very _____ with my room.
>
> W: What's _____ _____ the room?
>
> M: The air-conditioning is _____.

What's next?

(A) Can you check the room?

(B) We will send a man to fix it.

(C) They will be finished tomorrow.

(D) I would like to see the manager.

2.

> B: You _____ a bit _____.
>
> G: I _____ up _____ my boyfriend.
>
> B: Is there _____ I can do to _____ you?

What's next?

(A) That's too bad.

(B) No, she left already.

(C) I'm sorry to hear that.

(D) No, I'd like to be alone.

Unit Review

Listen and complete the dialogue. Track 3-3-8

 _____ are you crying John?

 I _____ _____ and broke my _____ truck.

 Don't be _____. I have a great idea!
Let's ask dad if he can _____ your truck.

 Don't worry, John. Your truck can be _____.

 I will fix it right away.
So, no more _____ _____... okay?

Okay···

 Here you go, John. Good _____ new!

Yay! _____ you dad!

 Listen. Pause. Say each sentence.

TOSEL 실전문제 ③

QR코드를 인식시키면
음원이 재생됩니다

1.

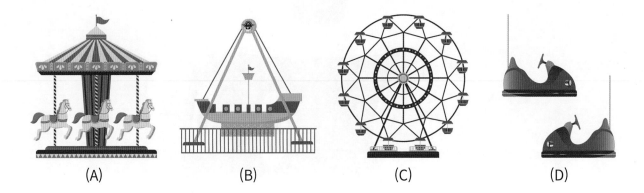

(A)　　　　　(B)　　　　　(C)　　　　　(D)

2.

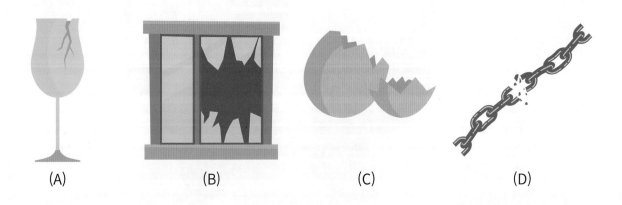

(A)　　　　　(B)　　　　　(C)　　　　　(D)

3.

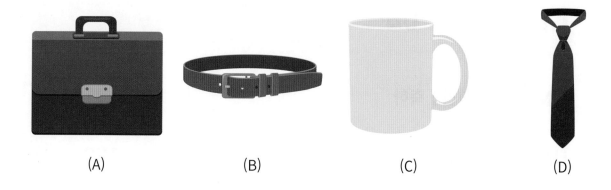

(A)　　　　　　(B)　　　　　　(C)　　　　　　(D)

4.

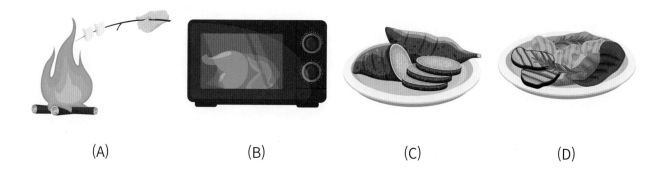

(A)　　　　　　(B)　　　　　　(C)　　　　　　(D)

5.

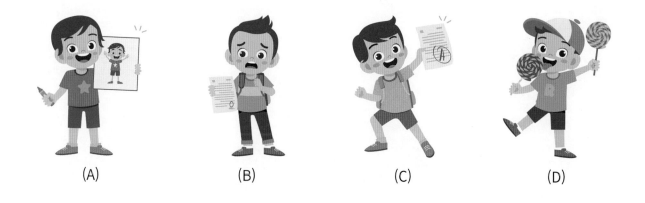

(A)　　　　　　(B)　　　　　　(C)　　　　　　(D)

CHAPTER 04

Unit 01

칭찬 / 축하

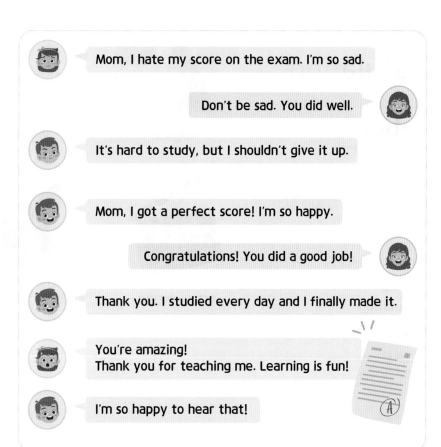

Mom, I hate my score on the exam. I'm so sad.

Don't be sad. You did well.

It's hard to study, but I shouldn't give it up.

Mom, I got a perfect score! I'm so happy.

Congratulations! You did a good job!

Thank you. I studied every day and I finally made it.

You're amazing!
Thank you for teaching me. Learning is fun!

I'm so happy to hear that!

congratulations (=congrats)	축하, 축하해(요)!	score	점수	mistake	실수
sports day	운동회	every day	매일	speech	연설, 강의
prize	상	finally	마침내, 마지막으로	hate	몹시 싫어하다
believe	믿다	wedding	결혼	practice	연습하다
perfect	완벽한	wonderful	아주 멋진, 훌륭한	make it	성공하다

Before Practice

Track 4-1-2

토셀쌤의 Sound Tip

• 어려운 발음

congratula<u>tion</u>

[-tion]

① [sh + n] 발음
② [-tion]은 단어를 **명사로 만들어주는** 역할을 하기도 한다.

option

emotion

congratulate 축하하다
↓
congratula<u>tion</u> 축하

act → ac<u>tion</u>

graduate → gradua<u>tion</u>

congratulation

Expressions. Listen and learn the expressions.

win a prize
상을 받다

do a good job
잘하다

make a mistake
실수를 하다

give up /give something up
포기하다

 **Practice**

 Track 4-1-3

Step 1. Listen to the words and write.

❶

❷

❸

❹

❺

❻

❼

❽

❾

❿

Step 2. Listen to the dialogue and fill in the blanks.

❶ **B**: _____ ! You _____ prize on sports day. You _____ it!

G: _____ ! I still can't _____ it myself!

❷ **B**: I couldn't get a _____ on the math exam.

G: You've studied so hard. You did a _____ !

Step 3. Complete the dialogue.

❶ **W**: Thank you for coming. I'm happy to see you here.

B: Aunt Jean, _____

❷ **G**: I made a big mistake in my speech. I hate myself!

B: Don't say that. _____

 Listen to the sentences and choose the best picture.

1.

> B : She _____ a good job in _____ the _____ .

(A) (B) (C) (D)

2.

> G : _____ ! _____ you all the best with the new _____ .

(A) (B) (C) (D)

Listen to the sentences and choose the best response.

1.

> **B**: I _____ an A on my _____ .
>
> **G**: _____ .

(A) Good _____ !

(B) Good _____ you!

(C) Best _____ from me.

(D) No, but _____ anyway.

2.

> **B**: Let me be the _____ to _____ you.
>
> **G**: _____ .

(A) Nice _____ !

(B) _____ work.

(C) Yes, help _____ .

(D) Thank you so _____ .

3.

> **B**: Did you _____ that we _____ first prize?
>
> **G**: _____ .

(A) They didn't work _____ .

(B) Happy _____ to you!

(C) Yes, I'm glad we _____ .

(D) No, he will _____ the game.

Listen to the short talks or conversations and choose the best answer.

1.

M: There's good _____ ! My wife _____ a _____ boy on Saturday.

W: Really? _____ on your _____ baby!

What are they celebrating?

(A)   (B)   (C)   (D)

2.

G: Congratulations _____ your _____ !

B: Thank you. I _____ can't _____ it _____ !

What are they celebrating?

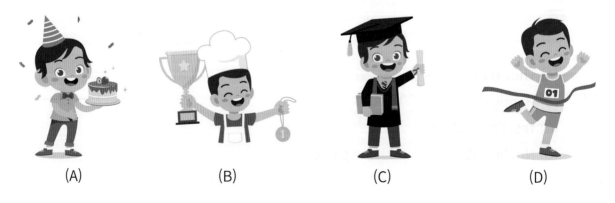

(A)   (B)   (C)   (D)

Listen to the conversations and choose the best response.

1.

> **B:** Look! I got a _____ score in the cooking _____ !
>
> **G:** Well _____ ! Was the challenge _____ ?
>
> **B:** Yes, but I _____ no _____ today.

What's next?

   (A) Sorry, that's too bad.

   (B) Congrats! You did it!

   (C) She's very good at it.

   (D) I'm worried about you.

2.

> **B:** _____ did your brother _____ in the marathon?
>
> **G:** He _____ in _____ .
>
> **B:** He _____ be a bit _____ right now.

What's next?

   (A) I heard the big news!

   (B) No, he was just lucky.

   (C) Yes, but I'm glad he didn't give up.

   (D) Nice job on coming in the first place!

UNIT 1 칭찬/축하

Unit Review

Listen and complete the dialogue.

Track 4-1-8

 Mom, I _____ my score on the exam. I'm so sad.

 Don't be sad. You _____ well.

 It's hard to study, but I shouldn't _____ it _____.

 Mom, I got a _____ score! I'm so happy.

 _____! You did a good _____!

 Thank you. I _____ every day and I finally _____ it.

 You're amazing! Thank you for _____ me.
Learning is _____!

 I'm so _____ to _____ that!

 Listen. Pause. Say each sentence.

Unit 02

의견 / 동의

Our class is going on a field trip next month. Tell me where you guys want to go.

I want to go skiing. It will be an exciting field trip in the beautiful winter.

I want to go to the aquarium. This winter will be very cold. We can catch a cold!

Okay, guys. We should vote. Vote for the place you want to go to.

field trip 현장 학습, 견학	**opinion** 의견	**cost** 비용이 들다	
aquarium 수족관	**agree** 동의하다, 찬성하다	**disagree** 반대하다	
vote 투표, 투표하다	**power** 힘	**better** 더 좋은, 나은	
temple stay 템플스테이	**personally** 개인적으로	**strongly** 강하게	
nature 자연	**school uniform** 교복	**save** 구하다, 절약하다	

Track 4-2-2

 토셀쌤의 Sound Tip

• **어려운 발음**

safe - save
life - live

f   v

leaf

leaves

① [f] 발음: [프-]하고 바람소리가 난다.
② [v]발음: [브~]하고 목이 떨리는 소리가 난다.

fan

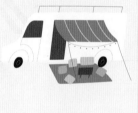
van

safe

Expressions. Listen and learn the expressions.

go on a field trip
현장 학습을 하다

catch a cold
감기에 걸리다

vote for/on
~을 위해 투표하다

agree/disagree with
~와 동의하다/
동의하지 않는다

Step 1. Listen to the words and write.

❶   ❻

❷   ❼

❸   ❽

❹   ❾

❺   ❿

Step 2. Listen to the dialogue and fill in the blanks.

❶ **G**: Our class is going on a   next month. We should go skiing.

     B: This winter will be very   . I   we should

                for a   stay!

❷ **G**: I   this   is   nature's   .

     B: I don't   . This movie is about the   of nature.

Step 3. Complete the dialogue.

❶ **B**: I personally believe that wearing a school uniform is important for all students.

     G:

❷ **B**: In my opinion, it is better to use paper bags than plastic bags.

     G:

 Listen to the sentences and choose the best picture.

1.

> **B** : I ⬜⬜⬜⬜ that too much ⬜⬜⬜⬜ is not good for your ⬜⬜⬜⬜ .

(A)

(B)

(C)

(D)

2.

> **G** : I ⬜⬜⬜⬜ we should ⬜⬜⬜⬜ ⬜⬜⬜⬜ and cans.

(A)

(B)

(C)

(D)

   Listen to the sentences and choose the best response.

1.

> **B**: I think this _____ is too _____ .
>
> **G**: _____ .

(A) Do you _____ help?

(B) It is _____ to me.

(C) I am _____ about that.

(D) Tell me _____ you want to go.

2.

> **B**: I feel that we should _____ into a new _____ .
>
> **G**: _____ .

(A) I like your new _____ .

(B) Where are you _____ ?

(C) I strongly _____ with you.

(D) I think our _____ is going to win.

3.

> **B**: Sometimes it is better to _____ .
>
> **G**: _____ .

(A) No _____ .

(B) Of _____ , I will.

(C) No, I don't _____ so.

(D) Don't _____ too much.

 Listen to the short talks or conversations and choose the best answer.

1.

> **B**: In my opinion, taking a taxi is ⬚⬚⬚ than taking a bus.
>
> **G**: No, I think we should take a bus. It is ⬚⬚⬚ now.

What are they going to take? Taxi or bus?

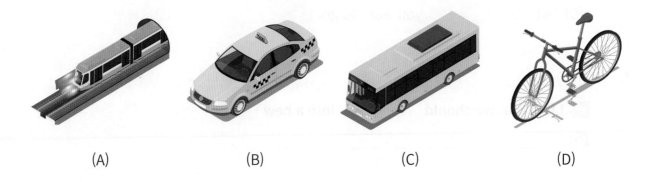

(A) (B) (C) (D)

2.

> **B**: I believe traveling will help you ⬚⬚⬚ about the world.
>
> **G**: Yes, I agree. But I think it is ⬚⬚⬚ to travel ⬚⬚⬚.

What are they agreeing on?

(A) (B) (C) (D)

 Listen to the conversations and choose the best response.

1.

> **B**: Jane says that she ⬚⬚⬚⬚ to go to the ⬚⬚⬚⬚ .
>
> **G**: But George ⬚⬚⬚⬚ me that he wanted to go to the ⬚⬚⬚⬚ .
>
> **B**: Well, what ⬚⬚⬚ we ⬚⬚⬚ now?

What's next?

 (A) Let's sing a song.

 (B) I think we should vote.

 (C) I will drive them to school.

 (D) I believe that she went home.

2.

> **B**: Can you ⬚⬚⬚⬚ more ⬚⬚⬚⬚ in the fireplace?
>
> **G**: Sure, ⬚⬚⬚⬚ will be much ⬚⬚⬚⬚ this year.
>
> **B**: I think we should ⬚⬚⬚⬚ more ⬚⬚⬚⬚ .

What's next?

 (A) I feel the same.

 (B) It's going to rain.

 (C) Please be quiet.

 (D) I felt so warm in that room.

Unit Review

Listen and complete the dialogue. Track 4-2-8

 Our class is going on a _____ trip next month.
Tell me _____ you guys want to go.

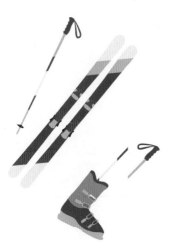

I want to go skiing.
It will be an _____ field trip
in the beautiful _____.

I want to go to the _____.
This winter will be very _____.
We can catch a cold!

 Okay, guys. We should _____.
Vote for the _____ you want to go to.

Listen. Pause. Say each sentence.

Unit 03

생각 / 견해

I don't like Halloween. The classroom looks scary.
Do you believe in ghosts?

Yes. I believe in ghosts.
Tomorrow is a day for ghosts.

Mom. I don't want to meet ghosts tomorrow.
Do you believe in ghosts?

Don't cry. People just dress up as ghosts.
You can also be a ghost.

Really? How can I be a ghost?

I'll tell you. What do you think about
wearing a costume for Halloween?
Then you will know all the ghosts are just people.
They are not real.

That sounds exciting! Maybe I can be a Dracula.

scary	무서운	relax	휴식하다	bright	밝은
dirty	더러운	costume	의상	culture	문화
ghost	귀신	sound	~인 것 같다	real	실제의
anymore	더이상	exciting	신나는, 흥미진진한	study abroad	유학하다
as a child	어릴 때	experience	경험	language	언어

Before Practice

Track 4-3-2

 토셀쌤의 Sound Tip

- 어려운 발음

d**ir**ty
cult**ur**e

| ir | er | ur |

각각 다르게 생겼지만
같은 소리가 난다.

circle

tiger

nurse

picture

dirty

Expressions. Listen and learn the expressions.

get dirty
더러워지다

relax at home
집에서 쉬다

believe in
~을 믿다

in my opinion
내 생각에는~

 **Practice**

Step 1. Listen to the words and write.

❶

❻

❷

❼

❸

❽

❹

❾

❺

❿

Step 2. Listen to the dialogue and fill in the blanks.

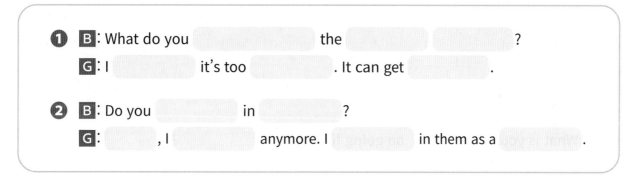

❶ **B**: What do you _____ the _____ _____ ?

G: I _____ it's too _____ . It can get _____ .

❷ **B**: Do you _____ in _____ ?

G: _____ , I _____ anymore. I _____ in them as a _____ .

Step 3. Complete the dialogue.

❶ **G**: _____

B: I like rainy weather. I can relax at home today.

❷ **G**: _____

B: In my experience, it's helpful to learn about a new culture and language.

 Listen to the sentences and choose the best picture.

1.

B : Do you _____ in Santa Claus?

(A)   (B)   (C)   (D)

2.

G : What is your _____ on going fishing this _____ ?

(A)   (B)   (C)   (D)

 Listen to the sentences and choose the best response.

1.

> **B**: How do you ⬚ about the ⬚ ?
>
> **G**: _____.

(A) I liked it ⬚ .

(B) Let's go to the ⬚ .

(C) I didn't really like the ⬚ .

(D) I think it is too ⬚ from here.

2.

> **B**: What's your ⬚ on ⬚ ?
>
> **G**: _____.

(A) I think I will go for a ⬚ .

(B) I don't ⬚ he exercised.

(C) I believe it is ⬚ for everyone.

(D) I couldn't believe it happened ⬚ .

3.

> **B**: Do you ⬚ in luck?
>
> **G**: _____.

(A) Yes, I ⬚ .

(B) No, I ⬚ not.

(C) No, you ⬚ .

(D) That sounds ⬚ .

 Listen to the short talks or conversations and choose the best answer.

1.

> B : What do you think about [   ] a [   ] ?
>
> G : No, I want to get a [   ] . I am [   ] to cats.

What type of pet does the girl want?

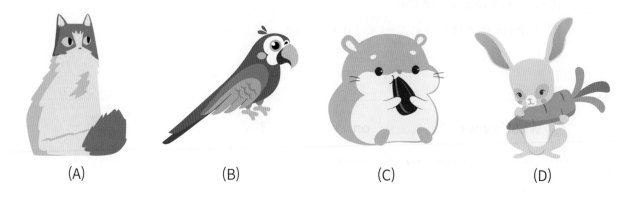

(A)   (B)   (C)   (D)

2.

> G : How do you feel [   ] my [   ] ?
>
> B : Great! I think long straight hair looks [   ] on you.

Which one is the girl's hairstyle?

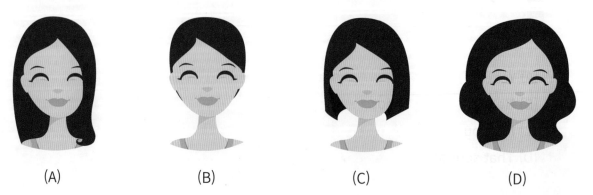

(A)   (B)   (C)   (D)

 Listen to the conversations and choose the best response.

1.

> **B**: ⬛⬛⬛⬛ do you think about my ⬛⬛⬛⬛ ?
>
> **G**: Oh, was it your ⬛⬛⬛⬛ gift?
>
> **B**: Yes. What's your opinion on the ⬛⬛⬛⬛ ?

What's next?

(A) In my opinion, she is smart.

(B) In my opinion, it is too early.

(C) In my opinion, you are wrong.

(D) In my opinion, it looks too dark.

2.

> **B**: All ⬛⬛⬛⬛ people are happy.
>
> **G**: Do you really ⬛⬛⬛⬛ so?
>
> **B**: Then, what is your ⬛⬛⬛⬛ about it?

What's next?

(A) I believe it will be beautiful.

(B) I think they also have bad days.

(C) I think it is easy to become famous.

(D) I really want to meet them personally.

Unit Review

Listen and complete the dialogue. ▶ Track 4-3-8

I don't like _____. The classroom looks _____.
Do you believe in ghosts?

Yes. I _____ in ghosts.
Tomorrow is a day for _____.

Mom. I don't want to _____ ghosts tomorrow.
Do you believe in ghosts?

Don't cry. People just _____ _____ as ghosts.
You can also be a ghost.

Really? _____ can I be a ghost?

I'll tell you.
What do you think about wearing a _____ for Halloween?
Then you will know all the ghosts are just people.
They are not _____.

That _____ exciting! Maybe I can be a Dracula.

Listen. Pause. Say each sentence.

TOSEL 실전문제 ④

QR코드를 인식시키면
음원이 재생됩니다

1.

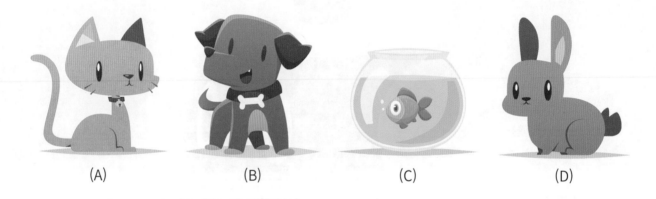

(A)　　　　　　　(B)　　　　　　　(C)　　　　　　　(D)

2.

(A)　　　　　　　(B)　　　　　　　(C)　　　　　　　(D)

3.

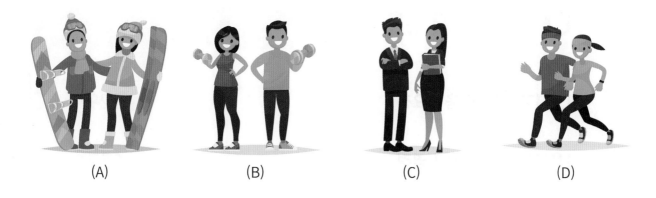

(A)　　　　　　(B)　　　　　　(C)　　　　　　(D)

4.

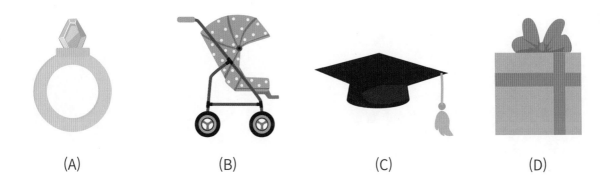

(A)　　　　　　(B)　　　　　　(C)　　　　　　(D)

5.

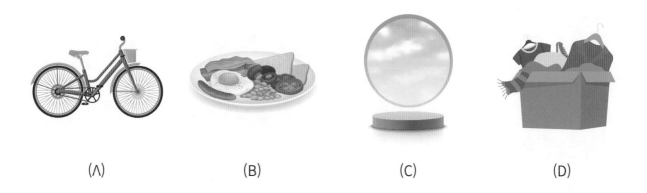

(A)　　　　　　(B)　　　　　　(C)　　　　　　(D)

CHAPTER 05

Unit 01

도움 / 요청

This box is too heavy for me to carry.

He must need a hand.

Excuse me,
could you give me a hand with this box?

Sure, I'm coming.

Thank you for your kind help.

I am glad to help.

I will lend you a hand next time
when you need my help.

Alright.

heavy	무거운	**carry**	운반하다	**need**	필요하다
kind	친절한	**classroom**	교실	**wake-up call**	모닝콜
lend	빌려주다	**get**	주다, 얻다	**handle**	다루다, 처리하다
next time	다음에	**bread**	빵	**own**	자신의, 직접 ~한
no problem	문제 없다, 괜찮다	**hand**	도움	**on my own (by myself)**	스스로

Before Practice

 토셀쌤의 Sound Tip

• 어려운 발음

ow**n** - t**ow**n

OW

[오우] 또는 [아우] 소리로 발음한다.

throw

shadow

powder

clown

Expressions. Listen and learn the expressions.

need a hand
도움이 필요하다

**give a hand
= lend a hand**
도움을 주다

why don't we~
~하는 게 어때

give a call
연락을 하다

Step 1. Listen to the words and write.

❶

❷

❸

❹

❺

❻

❼

❽

❾

❿

Step 2. Listen to the dialogue and fill in the blanks.

❶ G:　　　　　　me,　　　　　you　　　　　me, please?

　 B:　　　　　. No　　　　　. I can　　　　　three boxes for you.

❷ G:　　　　　　　　　　　we clean the　　　　　together?

　 B: Sounds　　　　　. But shouldn't you　　　　　home early today?

Step 3. Complete the dialogue.

❶ B:

　 G: I'd love it! How kind of you!

❷ B:

　 G: No, thank you. I'll handle it on my own.

 Listen to the sentences and choose the best picture.

1.

> **B**: Can _____ help me _____ this tree, _____ ?

(A)　　　　　　(B)　　　　　　(C)　　　　　　(D)

2.

> **G**: _____ you help me _____ my _____ ?

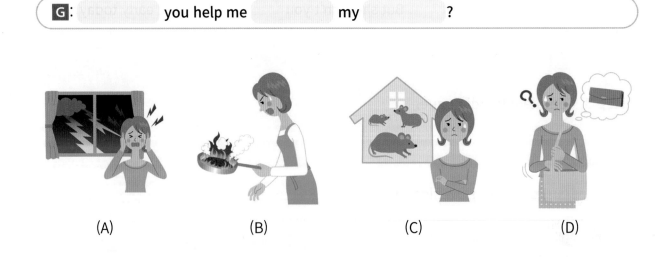

(A)　　　　　　(B)　　　　　　(C)　　　　　　(D)

 Listen to the sentences and choose the best response.

1.

> **B**: Can I _____ you _____ to eat?
>
> **G**: _____.

(A) You're _____ .

(B) That's too _____ .

(C) No, it's _____ .

(D) I would love _____ .

2.

> **B**: Could you help me _____ my father's _____ ?
>
> **G**: _____.

(A) Okay, that is _____ .

(B) I don't _____ your help.

(C) Can you give him a _____ ?

(D) _____ , what can I do for you?

3.

> **B**: Can you help me _____ my writing _____ , please?
>
> **G**: _____.

(A) That is not the right _____ .

(B) He is _____ with his homework.

(C) You should try It by _____ first.

(D) You should _____ to your teacher.

 Listen to the short talks or conversations and choose the best answer.

1.

M: _____ you like me to _____ you home?

W: No _____ . It's not _____ from here. I can _____ home.

How is the woman going home?

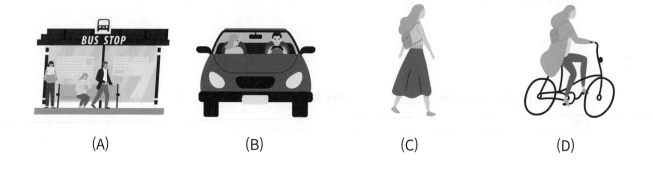

(A)   (B)   (C)   (D)

2.

B: Why don't we _____ paper bags _____ of _____ bags?

G: Sounds good! It will be _____ for _____ the earth.

What type of bag are they going to use?

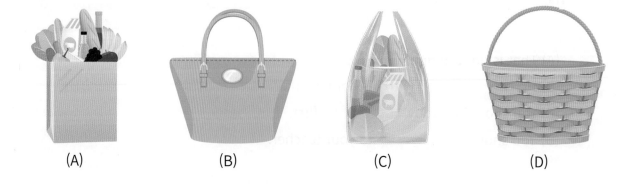

(A)   (B)   (C)   (D)

 Listen to the conversations and choose the best response.

1.

> B: Could you _____ me a _____ ?
>
> G: Sure, _____ can I help you _____ ?
>
> B: Could you _____ the _____ for a second?

What's next?

    (A) Here you are.

    (B) Of course, I can.

    (C) I will do it by myself.

    (D) I'm too busy right now.

2.

> B: Would you like me to _____ the _____ ?
>
> G: No, that's okay. I can do it _____ my _____ .
>
> B: You _____ do it. _____ me do it this time.

What's next?

    (A) It looks very nice.

    (B) Do you need a hand?

    (C) Okay, you are so kind.

    (D) Sorry, I have no time for that.

Unit Review

Listen and complete the dialogue.

▶ Track 5-1-8

This box is too _____ for me to _____.

He must _____ a _____.

Excuse me,
could you give me a _____ with this box?

Sure, I'm _____.

Thank you for your _____ help.

I am _____ to help.

I will _____ you a hand next time
when you need my help.

Alright.

Listen. Pause. Say each sentence.

Unit 02

▶ Track 5-2-1

걱정 / 염려

slip	미끄러지다	still	여전히	look for	찾다
worry	걱정하다	cheer up	힘내, 기운내	everywhere	모든 곳에
bandage	붕대	promise	약속	everything	모든 것
floor	바닥	knee	무릎	alright	괜찮은, 무사한
thrilled	신이 난	upset	속상한	miss	놓치다

Before Practice

 Track 5-2-2

 토셀쌤의 Sound Tip

- **어려운 발음**

<u>k</u>nee

K

[N] 앞의 [K]는 <u>발음하지 않는다.</u>

knife

knock

know

knight

Expressions. Listen and learn the expressions.

be worried about/for
~을 걱정하다

upset at
(someone or something)
속상해 하다

break one's promise
약속을 어기다

get someone down
~를 우울하게 만들다

 **Practice**

Step 1. Listen to the words and write.

❶

❷

❸

❹

❺

❻

❼

❽

❾

❿

Step 2. Listen to the dialogue and fill in the blanks.

❶ B: My knees   . I   on the   .

   G: You worried me. Here, I have a   .

❷ B: Tom was   at something. Is   ?

   G: He's still   . I   his   today.

Step 3. Complete the dialogue.

❶ G: We were worried about you.

   B: Sorry for making you worried. I just needed my own time.

❷ G: Are you alright?

   B: I worry about my parent's health. My dad had a heart attack a couple of days ago.

UNIT 2 걱정 / 염려

 Listen to the sentences and choose the best picture.

1.

G: I am _____ about my _____ .

(A) (B) (C) (D)

2.

B: I _____ _____ my English _____ tomorrow.

(A) (B) (C) (D)

Listen to the sentences and choose the best response.

1.

> B : Sorry, my phone _____ , so I couldn't _____ a _____ .
>
> G : _____ .

(A) Please _____ me.

(B) There's some in my _____ .

(C) I was _____ about you.

(D) Worrying too much isn't _____ .

2.

> B : I _____ my _____ on the tree in _____ of your house.
>
> G : _____ .

(A) Are you _____ ?

(B) Don't be _____ .

(C) Are you _____ ?

(D) Everything is _____ .

3.

> M : I _____ about the car _____ . Are you _____ ?
>
> W : _____ .

(A) Oh, that is _____ .

(B) No, I feel _____ .

(C) Yes, I am very _____ .

(D) I hope you are feeling _____ .

UNIT 2 걱정 / 염려

 Listen to the short talks or conversations and choose the best answer.

1.

> **M**: Is _____ alright? You look so _____.
>
> **W**: My _____ won't stop _____ mobile _____.

What is the woman worrying about?

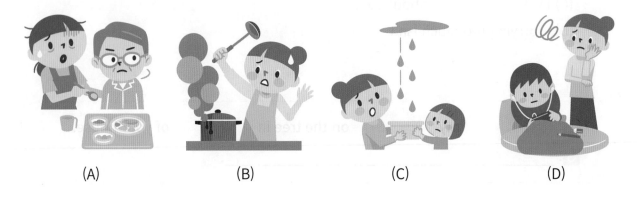

(A)   (B)   (C)   (D)

2.

> **B**: Drink more _____ ! I'm very _____ about your _____.
>
> **G**: Okay. From now on, I will _____ 2 liters of _____ a day.

What is the boy worrying about?

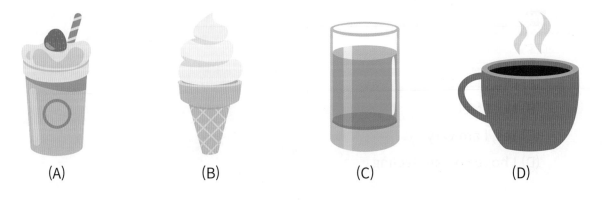

(A)   (B)   (C)   (D)

 Listen to the conversations and choose the best response.

1.

> **B**: What's   ? You look so   .
>
> **G**: I'm   about tomorrow's   .
>
> **B**: Don't worry.   is   to be okay.

What's next?

(A) Don't give up yet.

(B) You look very tired.

(C) That's very kind of you.

(D) The concert is finally over.

2.

> **B**: Are you   ? What is   you down?
>
> **G**: I had a   . I said harsh   to Mary.
>
> **B**: Why   you say   to her first?

What's next?

(A) I'm so sorry.

(B) Yes, I agree.

(C) Oh, is it true?

(D) Yes, I'm okay

Unit Review

Listen and complete the dialogue. (▶) Track 5-2-8

I am so _____ about the _____ game tomorrow.
I just can't _____.

Are you _____, John?

I _____ on the wet floor.

Oh, no! I think I _____ my leg.

I'm _____ about you.
Let's go to the hospital.

Cheer up buddy!
Don't be _____ about missing the soccer match.
There's _____ next time.

 Listen. Pause. Say each sentence.

Unit 03

제안 / 초대

 It's finally Friday.
What are you doing over the weekend?

Not sure.
How about watching a movie together?

 Great plan. Do you have something in mind?

Superhero movies, of course!

 Let me also ask Sophia
if she can come with us to the theater.

 She will be glad to come.

 Thank you for inviting me, but I can't.
I have to study for an exam.

 That's too bad. Well then, next time.

plan	계획	**mind**	마음, 정신	**theater**	극장
superhero	슈퍼히어로	**glad**	기쁜	**exam**	시험
invite	초대하다	**holiday**	휴가, 연휴	**offer**	제의
throw	(파티를) 벌이다, 열다	**book**	예약하다	**welcome**	환영하다
ticket	표, 티켓	**suggestion**	제안	**teammate**	팀 동료

Before Practice

 토셀쌤의 Sound Tip

• 어려운 발음

th**row** - **th**ere

th

① th[ㅆ]: 혀를 이 사이로 내보내고 공기를 내보낸다.
② th[ㄷ]: 혀를 이 사이로 내보내고 성대를 울린다.

thea**t**er

thief

mo**th**er

they

throw

Expressions. Listen and learn the expressions.

throw a party
파티를 열다

have something in mind
~을 생각해 놓다

make suggestion
제안을 하다

be on time
시간을 맞추다

Step 1. Listen to the words and write.

❶ _____

❷ _____

❸ _____

❹ _____

❺ _____

❻ _____

❼ _____

❽ _____

❾ _____

❿ _____

Step 2. Listen to the dialogue and fill in the blanks.

❶ G : What should we do for the holidays? Do you have _____ ?

B : How about going to Jeju island?
    I can _____ the _____ for you.

❷ G : Can I make a _____ for _____'s dinner?

B : Yes, what _____ you _____ to eat?

Step 3. Complete the dialogue.

❶ B : Why don't you come to the party today at 7 o'clock?

G : _____

❷ B : _____ You are welcome to come.

G : Thank you for the offer, but I have to study for an exam.

 Listen to the sentences and choose the best picture.

1.

G: Would you like to _____ our _____ team?

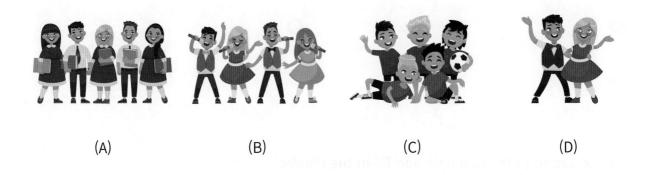

(A)　　　　　　　　(B)　　　　　　　　(C)　　　　　　　　(D)

2.

B: _____ don't we _____ a _____ together?

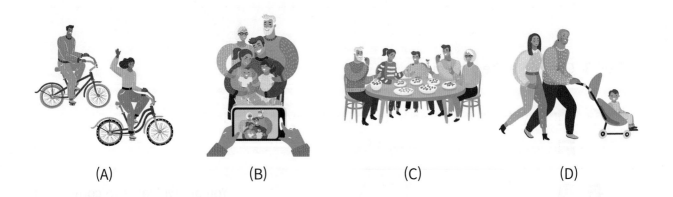

(A)　　　　　　　　(B)　　　　　　　　(C)　　　　　　　　(D)

Listen to the sentences and choose the best response.

1.

> **B**: Would you like _____ to _____ ?
>
> **G**: _____ .

(A) No, it is _____ .

(B) I don't drink _____ .

(C) Yes, I'll have iced _____ .

(D) Three hot dogs, _____ .

2.

> **B**: _____ you like to _____ a little longer?
>
> **G**: _____ .

(A) We'd _____ to do that.

(B) We'll be there _____ .

(C) Thank you for _____ me.

(D) I don't have anything in _____ .

3.

> **B**: I can't _____ the _____ for the dinner.
>
> **G**: _____ .

(A) He _____ me to have dinner.

(B) I _____ have a big dinner.

(C) What is your _____ ?

(D) Can I make a _____ ?

UNIT 3 제안 / 초대

 Listen to the short talks or conversations and choose the best answer.

1.

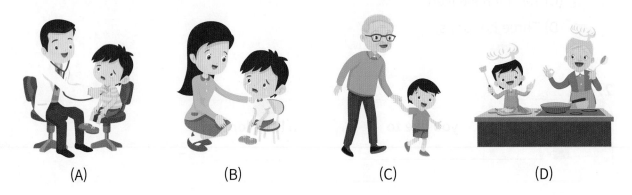

B: I think I _____ a _____. _____ should I do?

G: _____ about going to the _____?

What is the boy going to do?

(A) (B) (C) (D)

2.

B: Would you like to play _____ with _____?

G: Thanks for the _____, but I have a _____ this afternoon.

What is the girl going to do?

(A) (B) (C) (D)

 Listen to the conversations and choose the best response.

1.

> **B**: Do you want to go _____ with us _____ Saturday?
>
> **G**: I'm so sorry. We will be _____ _____ then.
>
> **B**: Well, _____ about _____ Saturday?

What's next?

   (A) Sounds good.

   (B) It's Friday today.

   (C) When are you free?

   (D) Let's boil some eggs.

2.

> **B**: Let's _____ something to _____ our mom.
>
> **G**: For a Christmas gift? Do you have _____ in _____ ?
>
> **B**: I got an _____ . How about _____ ?

What's next?

   (A) That's too bad.

   (B) That's a good idea.

   (C) I'm not feeling well.

   (D) I forgot your birthday.

Unit Review

Listen and complete the dialogue. Track 5-3-8

 It's _____ Friday.
What are you doing _____ the weekend?

Not sure.
How about _____ a movie together?

 Great plan. Do you have something in _____?

Superhero movies, of _____!

 Let me _____ ask Sophia
if she can _____ with us to the theater.

 She will be _____ to come.

 Thank you for _____ me, but I can't.
I have to _____ for an exam.

 That's too _____. Well then, next time.

🔊 Listen. Pause. Say each sentence.

TOSEL 실전문제 ⑤

QR코드를 인식시키면
음원이 재생됩니다

1.

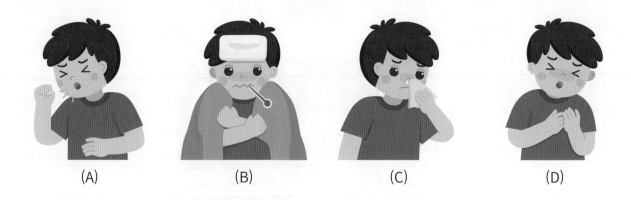

(A)　　　　　(B)　　　　　(C)　　　　　(D)

2.

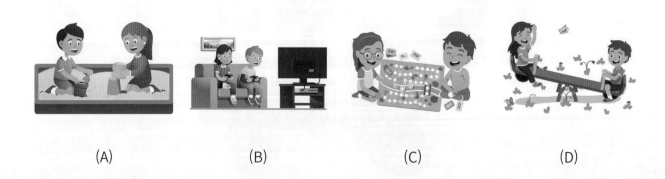

(A)　　　　　(B)　　　　　(C)　　　　　(D)

3.

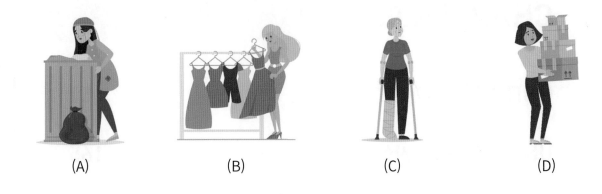

(A)   (B)   (C)   (D)

4.

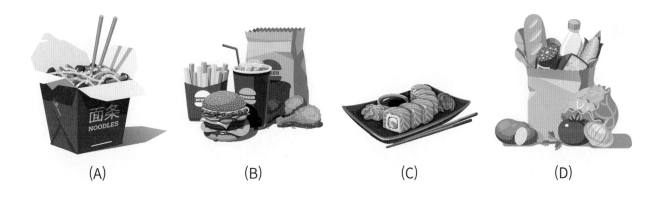

(A)   (B)   (C)   (D)

5.

(A)   (B)   (C)   (D)

CHAPTER 06

Unit 01

소식 / 전달

 Let's take out the trash together, Charlie. Now, we finished cleaning our house!

 Oh my… What is this mess? I don't see any footprints anywhere. It must be a monster.

Did you hear that there is a monster in our town?

 What? Someone made a big mess last night near the garbage bin.

Woof! Woof!

 Oh no... It's that monster again.

 Wait, that's Charlie barking. So, you were responsible for all this? Charlie!

mess	엉망	**responsible**	책임이 있는	**pollution**	오염
woof	개가 크게 짖는 소리	**trash**	쓰레기	**surprise**	놀라움
bark	짖다	**footprint**	발자국	**throw**	(파티를) 열다
reduce	줄이다	**strict**	엄격한	**schedule**	계획, 스케줄
monster	괴물	**garbage**	쓰레기	**bin**	쓰레기통

Before Practice

Track 6-1-2

 토셀쌤의 Sound Tip

- **어려운 발음**

sc**h**edule / **ch**eese / wat**ch**

ch

① [ㅋ]: 그리스어에서 유래한 단어는 [ch]를 [ㅋ]로 발음한다.
② [ㅊ]: 이외에는 대체로 [ch]를 [ㅊ]로 발음한다.
③ [치]: 단어가 [ch]로 끝날 때는 [-치]로 발음한다.

christmas

character

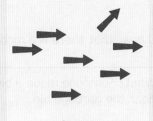
change

swit**ch**

schedule

Expressions. Listen and learn the expressions.

hear the news
소식을 듣다

make a mess
어질러 놓다

be responsible for
책임이 있다

talk about
~에 대해 이야기하다

Step 1. Listen to the words and write.

1   **6**

2   **7**

3   **8**

4   **9**

5   **10**

Step 2. Listen to the dialogue and fill in the blanks.

1 **B**: James   me that Jackson's   is this   .

 G: Then, we should   him a   birthday party.

2 **B**: Will you   Dean about tomorrow's work schedule?

 G: Yes, I am   him this   .

Step 3. Complete the dialogue.

1 **G**:

 B: Yes, I heard that he is very strict.

2 **W**: What is the topic for the next meeting?

 M:

UNIT 1 소식 / 전달

Listen to the sentences and choose the best picture.

1.

G : My _____ told me that _____ are good for your _____ .

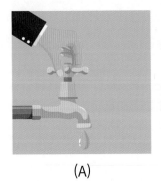

(A)

(B)

(C)

(D)

2.

B : Today, I am going to _____ about _____ to save _____ .

(A)

(B)

(C)

(D)

 Listen to the senctences and choose the best response.

1.

> **B**: What is your   for today's   ?
>
> **G**: _____.

(A) We can't hear you   .

(B) I am not   talk to him.

(C) I will talk about my   .

(D) This is the   of my presentation.

2.

> **B**:   you   Noah about tomorrow's party?
>
> **G**: _____.

(A) No, he said   about it.

(B)   will you tell him about it?

(C) Come on, the party   soon.

(D) Sure, I will tell him on my   home.

3.

> **M**: Did you   that James   with Sophia?
>
> **W**: _____.

(A) Shhh! He might   .

(B) Oh! It must be very   .

(C) Please don't   me alone.

(D) Come on! You know the   .

UNIT 1 소식 / 전달

 Listen to the short talks or conversations and choose the best answer.

1.

B: Oliver [_____] me that we can see [_____] [_____] today.

G: Let's go out then. I will [_____] my [_____].

What are they going to see tonight?

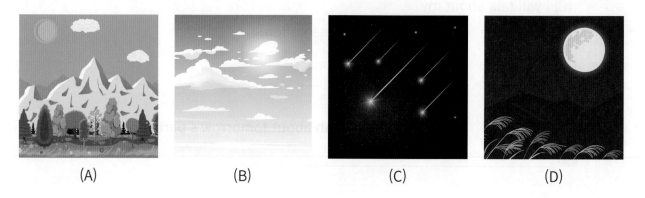

(A)   (B)   (C)   (D)

2.

M: Did you hear that Emma is [_____] [_____]? Do you [_____] the date?

W: Yes, the [_____] is on [_____] 17th.

When is Emma's wedding?

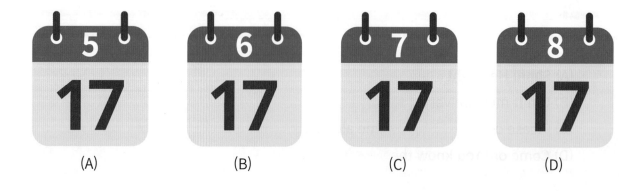

(A)   (B)   (C)   (D)

 Listen to the conversations and choose the best response.

1.

> **B**: How was the English ⬚ ⬚ ?
>
> **G**: I got a B on it. I ⬚ a few ⬚ .
>
> **B**: That's not ⬚ bad. When ⬚ you tell your ⬚ about it?

What's next?

(A) I'll tell them tonight.

(B) I can't talk right now.

(C) I didn't take the test.

(D) I'll tell you my secret.

2.

> **B**: Hello, Mrs. Kim. Did you ⬚ me?
>
> **W**: Yes, ⬚ you tell your parents ⬚ the field ⬚ ?
>
> **B**: Oh, no. Sorry, I ⬚ to tell them ⬚ .

What's next?

(A) She doesn't want to talk to me.

(B) She is very strict with her children.

(C) Then, don't forget to tell them today.

(D) It's all right, but I prefer watching movies.

Unit Review

Listen and complete the dialogue.

Track 6-1-8

 Let's take out the trash _____ Charlie.
Now, we _____ cleaning our house!

 Oh my··· What is this mess?
I don't see any _____ anywhere.
It must be a _____.

Did you hear that there is a _____ in our town?

 What? Someone _____ a big _____
last night near the _____ bin.

Woof! Woof!

 Oh no... It's that monster _____.

 Wait, that's Charlie _____.
So, you were _____ _____ all this? Charlie!

 Listen. Pause. Say each sentence.

Unit 02

확인 / 사실

Jack,
finish your homework before you go to the park.
I will check them
after I come back from the groceries.

Okay, I will.

Oh no, I broke the window.
What am I going to do..? I should stay quiet.

Jack, don't you have anything to say?
I won't get mad if you tell the truth.

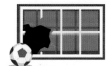

To be honest, I broke the window.

I'm sorry, mom. It was a mistake.

It's okay. Thank you for being honest.

groceries	슈퍼마켓	**truth**	사실	**quiet**	조용한
mistake	실수	**check**	확인하다	**anything**	무엇이든
mad	화가 난	**honest**	솔직한	**present**	선물(=gift)
truthfully	진실하게	**at all**	전혀, 조금도	**finish**	끝내다
photocopy	복사	**happen**	발생하다, 일어나다	**nothing**	아무것도

Before Practice

 Track 6-2-2

 토셀쌤의 Sound Tip

• **어려운 발음**

happen / English

en

① [은] : 단어 끝에 올 때, 앞의 자음과 함께 소리 낸다.

② [인, 잉] : 주로 단어 맨 앞에 올 때

garden

listen

enjoy

envy

happen

Expressions. Listen and learn the expressions.

tell the truth
사실을 말하다

in truth
솔직히 말하면

be honest
솔직하다

look good on
~에게 잘 어울리다

 **Practice**

Step 1. Listen to the words and write.

❶

❻

❷

❼

❸

❽

❹

❾

❺

❿

Step 2. Listen to the dialogue and fill in the blanks.

❶ B: Did she _____ the _____ we gave her on her birthday?

G: In _____ , she was not happy at all.

❷ B: _____ you _____ doing your homework?

G: To be _____ , I didn't _____ my homework for today.

Step 3. Complete the dialogue.

❶ G: _____

B: Truthfully, I don't think it looks good on you.

❷ G: _____

B: To be honest, I was taking a shower with loud music on.

So, I don't know anything.

 Track 6-2-4

 Listen to the sentences and choose the best picture.

1.

B: To be _____ , I _____ most of the _____ last night.

(A)　　　　　　　　(B)　　　　　　　　(C)　　　　　　　　(D)

2.

G: _____ , I went _____ with some _____ .

(A)　　　　　　　　(B)　　　　　　　　(C)　　　　　　　　(D)

 Listen to the sentences and choose the best response.

1.

> B : You shouldn't ⬚⬚⬚ your friend's ⬚⬚⬚ .
>
> G : _____ .

(A) She ⬚⬚⬚ this.

(B) Well done! There is no ⬚⬚⬚ .

(C) In truth, I didn't ⬚⬚⬚ my lunch.

(D) In truth, I ⬚⬚⬚ the homework.

2.

> B : What do you ⬚⬚⬚ of my new ⬚⬚⬚ ?
>
> G : _____ .

(A) To be honest, I think she's ⬚⬚⬚ .

(B) To be honest, I spent all of the ⬚⬚⬚ .

(C) To be honest, it doesn't ⬚⬚⬚ good on you.

(D) To be honest, it ran away ⬚⬚⬚ you came.

3.

> B : Are you ⬚⬚⬚ for tomorrow's ⬚⬚⬚ ?
>
> G : _____ .

(A) Well, I didn't finish my ⬚⬚⬚ .

(B) In truth, he ⬚⬚⬚ all day studying.

(C) Don't tell me that you ⬚⬚⬚ it again.

(D) Truthfully, I didn't read the book ⬚⬚⬚ .

 Listen to the short talks or conversations and choose the best answer.

1.

> **B**: Oh, no! What _____ to my _____ ?
>
> **G**: I am very sorry. In _____ , my _____ brother _____ it.

What happened to the boy?

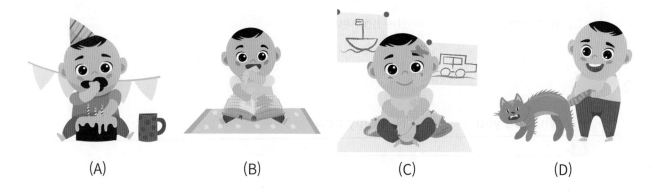

(A)   (B)   (C)   (D)

2.

> **B**: The movie was _____ ! I love the main _____ .
>
> **G**: Well, to be _____ , I don't _____ like _____ movies.

What movie did they watch together?

(A)   (B)   (C)   (D)

 Listen to the conversations and choose the best response.

1.

> B: What's with a 　　　　　　 　　　　　　 ?
>
> G: I just 　　　　　　 my essay 　　　　　　 for this week.
>
> B: Oh, in 　　　　　　 , the essay is 　　　　　　 next week.

What's next?

(A) In truth, he never tells a lie.

(B) No, I can't finish this on time.

(C) Really? Why didn't you tell me?

(D) Don't you have anything to say?

2.

> B: The class is finally 　　　　　　 . Let's go home 　　　　　　 .
>
> G: How was 　　　　　　 class? Wasn't it 　　　　　　 ?
>
> B: To be honest, I couldn't 　　　　　　 today's 　　　　　　 .

What's next?

(A) I would like to join a sports club.

(B) Be quiet please. I'm on the phone.

(C) Don't worry. I can teach you again.

(D) How about taking a history class?

Unit Review

Listen and complete the dialogue. Track 6-2-8

Jack,
_____ your _____ before you go to the park.
I will _____ them after I come back
from the _____.

Okay, I will.

 Oh no, I _____ the window.
What am I going to do..? I should _____ quiet.

 Jack, don't you have _____ to say?
I won't get mad if you tell the _____.

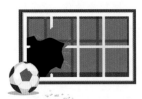

To be _____, I broke the window.

I'm sorry, mom. It was a _____.

 It's okay. Thank you for _____ honest.

 Listen. Pause. Say each sentence.

Unit 03

일정 / 계획

 What are you going to do during summer vacation?

I am traveling abroad. I am flying to Canada.

 Wow, that's great.
How long are you staying in Canada for?

 I am thinking of staying there for a week.

My uncle moved to Toronto
and this is my first time visiting him there.

 I see. So, you must be visiting many places then.

I am excited about seeing the CN tower
and having maple syrup.

 Hope you enjoy it and have a safe trip!

vacation	방학, 휴가	**visit**	방문하다	**plenty**	충분히
stay	머물다, 지내다	**have**	먹다	**file**	파일, 서류파일
travel	여행하다	**safe**	안전한	**after**	~뒤에, 후에
abroad	해외로	**due~**	~할 예정인, 예정된	**volleyball**	배구
fly	비행하다, 비행기를 타다	**assignment**	과제	**extra**	여분의

Before Practice

 토셀쌤의 Sound Tip

• **어려운 발음**

assignment

g

[N] 앞의 [G]는 발음하지 않는다.

sign

design

campaign

foreign

schedule

Expressions. Listen and learn the expressions.

travel abroad
해외여행을 가다

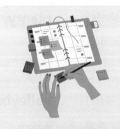
have a plan
계획이 있다

have something
~을 먹다

plenty of time
충분한 시간

Practice

Step 1. Listen to the words and write.

❶

❻

❷

❼

❸

❽

❹

❾

❺

❿

Step 2. Listen to the dialogue and fill in the blanks.

❶ **G**: When is the   date for this   ?

  B: It is due next Friday. You have   of   .

❷ **G**: Do you know where my laptop is?

  B: It's in my   the   .

Step 3. Complete the dialogue.

❶ **G**:

  B: Yes, I am going to travel abroad for two weeks.

❷ **G**:

  B: Just bring extra clothes to change after beach volleyball.

 Listen to the sentences and choose the best picture.

1.

B : A _____ is sitting _____ a tree.

(A)　　　　　　　(B)　　　　　　　(C)　　　　　　　(D)

2.

G : My _____ for summer _____ is learning how to play _____ .

(A)　　　　　　　(B)　　　　　　　(C)　　　　　　　(D)

Listen to the senctences and choose the best response.

1.

M : **When is the**   **date for the**   **?**

W : _____ .

(A) It is   next Monday.

(B) The bus will   at six.

(C) We began the   in May.

(D) I finally   reading this book.

2.

B : **How**   **do you come here for**   **?**

G : _____ .

(A) Never, I do not like   .

(B)   ten minutes. So, let's wait.

(C) Not very   . This is my   time.

(D) It   ten hours to
from Seoul to Sydney.

3.

B : **How**   **are you going to**   **in Australia?**

G : _____ .

(A) Would you like to   with me?

(B) I'll   money to go to Australia.

(C) I am thinking of   for a month.

(D) It   me three   to pack my bag.

 Listen to the short talks or conversations and choose the best answer.

1.

> **G**: What do I need to _____ for the swimming _____ ?
>
> **B**: _____ a swimming _____ , swimming _____ and goggles.

What do you NOT need for the swimming lesson?

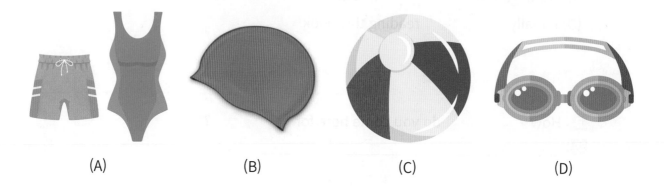

(A)　　　　　　(B)　　　　　　(C)　　　　　　(D)

2.

> **G**: Do you have any plans for _____ ?
>
> **B**: Yes, I am going to _____ the _____ on the top of a _____ .

What is the boy going to do on January 1st?

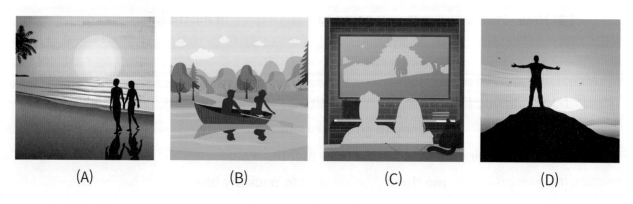

(A)　　　　　　(B)　　　　　　(C)　　　　　　(D)

 Listen to the conversations and choose the best response.

1.

> **B**: When is the due   for the   presentation?
>
> **G**: The presentation is due   .
>
> **B**: Let's   up. By the way, did you see my   ?

What's next?

(A) You are going too fast.

(B) I told him about the contest.

(C) It is beside my laptop on the desk.

(D) There's something beneath the water.

2.

> **B**: Do you   the   for Ella's birthday?
>
> **G**: She   me that it is on   2nd.
>
> **B**: I see. What will you   for her   ?

What's next?

(A) I want you to be happy.

(B) I'll make a candle for her.

(C) I don't want you to bring any food.

(D) In truth, she didn't really like the present.

Unit Review

Listen and complete the dialogue.

 What are you going to do _____ summer _____?

 I am traveling _____. I am flying to Canada.

 Wow, that's great.
_____ long are you staying in Canada for?

 I am thinking of staying there for a _____.

 My uncle _____ _____ Toronto and this is my first time _____ him there.

 I see. So, you _____ be visiting many places then.

 I am _____ about seeing the CN tower and having _____ syrup.

 Hope you _____ it and have a safe trip!

 Listen. Pause. Say each sentence.

TOSEL 실전문제 ⑥

QR코드를 인식시키면
음원이 재생됩니다

SECTION I. Listening and Speaking

In SECTION I, you will be asked to demonstrate how well you understand spoken English. You will have approximately 5 minutes to complete this section.

SECTION I은 듣기 능력을 평가합니다.

PART A. Listen and Recognize

DIRECTIONS: For questions 1 to 5, listen to the sentences and choose the BEST picture. The sentences will be spoken **TWICE.**

지시 사항: 1번부터 5번까지는 문장을 듣고, 가장 알맞은 그림을 고르는 문제입니다. 문제는 **두 번씩** 들려줍니다.

1.

(A)　　　　　　(B)　　　　　　(C)　　　　　　(D)

2.

(A)　　　　　　(B)　　　　　　(C)　　　　　　(D)

3.

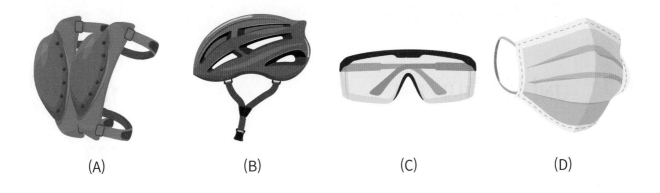

(A)   (B)   (C)   (D)

4.

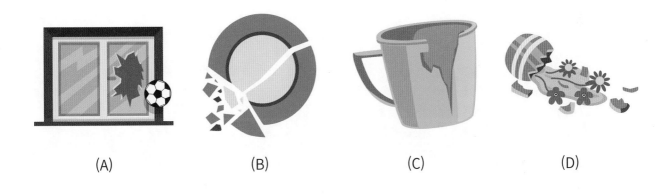

(A)   (B)   (C)   (D)

5.

(A)   (B)   (C)   (D)

CHAPTER 07

Unit 01

지시 / 허락

 Class, what are the rules for using the library?

We have to be quiet.

No running is allowed.

 That's right!
Just follow the rules and you will be fine.

 John, what were the rules
you have to follow in the library?

No talking and no running in the hallway...

 Sit down and think what you've done, John.

Yes, Ms. Smith.

rule	규칙	**hallway**	복도	**ballpark**	야구장
have to	~해야하다 (=need to)	**library**	도서관	**chores**	집안일
allow	용납하다	**action**	행동	**forget**	잊다 (forget-forgot-forgotten)
follow	따라가다, 따르다	**answer**	답, 정답	**dish**	접시
instruction	지시	**copy**	베끼다	**wash**	씻다

Before Practice

Track 7-1-2

 토셀쌤의 Sound Tip

• **어려운 발음**

w<u>r</u>ite / <u>wh</u>o / an<u>sw</u>er

W

[W : 소리 없음]

① [w] 뒤에 [r]이 있는 경우
② [w] 뒤에 [h]가 있는 경우
③ [s] 뒤에 [w]가 있는 경우

wrong

wrap

whole

sword

write

Expressions. Listen and learn the expressions.

do dishes
설거지를 하다

do chores
집안일을 하다

write down
~을 적다

take a walk
산책을 하다

 **Practice**

Step 1. Listen to the words and write.

❶

❻

❷

❼

❸

❽

❹

❾

❺

❿

Step 2. Listen to the dialogue and fill in the blanks.

❶ **G**: Let me   Jane's answers.

  B: You   your friend's homework.

❷ **G**: What do I   to do after   today?

  B: You   to take the dog for a   .

Step 3. Complete the dialogue.

❶ **G**: Can I go to the ballpark after lunch?

  M:

❷ **W**:

  B: Mom, can I wash them after I come back?

UNIT 1 지시 / 허락

 Listen to the sentences and choose the best picture.

1.

G: When you _____ the room, turn _____ the _____.

(A)   (B)   (C)   (D)

2.

B: Do not take _____ in the _____.

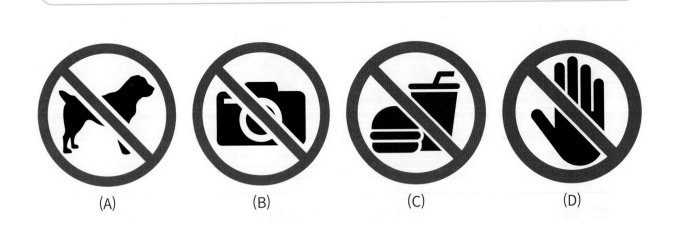

(A)   (B)   (C)   (D)

 Listen to the sentences and choose the best response.

1.

> B: _____ _____ ! You're _____ on my foot.
>
> G: _____ .

(A) You're really _____ .

(B) Oh, sorry. I didn't _____ .

(C) I can't _____ your order.

(D) No problem. I do it _____ .

2.

> B: Can I go _____ and _____ with my friends?
>
> W: _____ .

(A) Yes, I will help you _____ .

(B) Yes, I _____ get some rest.

(C) No, you _____ finish your lunch.

(D) No, they are going to _____ singing.

3.

> B: Don't _____ to brush your teeth _____ sleeping.
>
> G: _____ .

(A) _____ , you can have it.

(B) No! I _____ my car key.

(C) Don't _____ , I will do it.

(D) No, I _____ have one.

 Listen to the short talks or conversations and choose the best answer.

1.

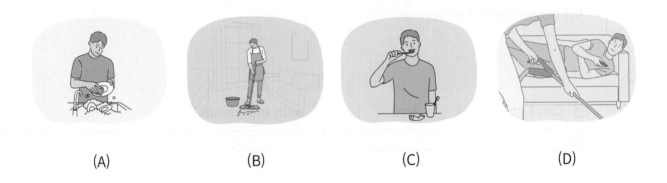

B: The house is a _____ ! I think we _____ _____ clean up.

G: Do the _____ . I will clean the _____ .

What does the boy have to do for cleaning?

(A)   (B)   (C)   (D)

2.

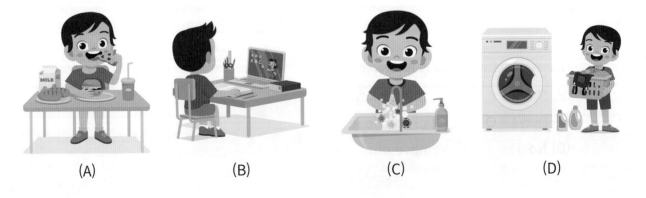

B: Wow, you _____ a pizza! Can I have a _____ ?

G: _____ your hands _____ . And then, _____ some napkins.

What does the boy need to do first?

(A)   (B)   (C)   (D)

 Listen to the conversations and choose the best response.

1.

> **B** : Hey, Lucy.   is Mary? Is she not   well?
>
> **G** : Mary can't go to the   . Let's   now.
>
> **B** :   isn't she   ?

What's next?

   (A) I need to return this book.

   (B) Her parents can't go to China.

   (C) She cleaned her car this morning.

   (D) She has to look after her sister tonight.

2.

> **M** : What   do you have to   during the exam?
>
> **G** : First, don't   your friend's   .
>
> **M** : That's   . Can you tell me   ?

What's next?

   (A) You need to have breakfast.

   (B) You can talk in the exam room.

   (C) You can't use your mobile phone.

   (D) You should write on the exam desk.

UNIT 1 지시 / 허락

Unit Review

Listen and complete the dialogue. Track 7-1-8

 Class, what are the _____ for using the library?

We have to be _____.

No running is _____.

 That's right!
Just _____ the _____ and you will be fine.

 John, what were the rules
you have to follow in the _____?

No talking and no running in the _____...

 Sit down and _____ what you've done, John.

Yes, Ms. Smith.

 Listen. Pause. Say each sentence.

Unit 02

조언 / 충고

▶ Track 7-2-1

 What are some of the road safety rules you know?

No crossing at a redlight.

 You are correct. You shouldn't cross at a redlight.

No jaywalking. You must cross only at crosswalks.

You should wear a helmet when you are on a bike.

 You are all correct!
Watch out for cars, pay attention to the lights,
and be careful when crossing the road.

helmet	헬멧	**light**	신호등	**safety**	안전
crosswalk	횡단보도	**cross**	건너다	**careful**	조심하는
jaywalking	무단 횡단	**road**	도로	**wear**	착용하다
bike	자전거	**attention**	주의	**send**	보내다
text	문자 메시지	**souvenir**	기념품	**place**	장소

Before Practice

 Track 7-2-2

 토셀쌤의 Sound Tip

• **어려운 발음**

crosswalk<u>s</u> / road<u>s</u> / wash<u>es</u>

 s **es**

① s - : 성대가 울리지 않는 자음 뒤에 올 때
② s - : 성대가 울리는 자음 뒤에 올 때
③ es - : 단어가 -s, -ss, -sh, -ch, -x 로
　　　　 끝날 때

stop<u>s</u>

toy<u>s</u>

watch<u>es</u>

fix<u>es</u>

crosswalks

Expressions. Listen and learn the expressions.

cross the road
길을 건너다

on a bike
자전거에 타 있다

pay attention
주의를 하다

watch out
조심하다

Practice

Track 7-2-3

Step 1. Listen to the words and write.

❶

❷

❸

❹

❺

❻

❼

❽

❾

❿

Step 2. Listen to the dialogue and fill in the blanks.

❶ **G**: What is   this   , John?

     B: Be   with that, it's a   from Scotland.

❷ **G**: I will just do my   .

     B: I   you, I would do it right now.

Step 3. Complete the dialogue.

❶ **M**: Let me send him a text message.

     W:

❷ **B**: Mom, I'm going to Mike's place. I will be back at 6.

     W:

UNIT 2 조언 / 충고

Basic 195

 Listen to the sentences and choose the best picture.

1.

G: [   ] out for [   ] animals on the [   ].

(A)　　　　　　(B)　　　　　　(C)　　　　　　(D)

2.

B: Be [   ]! I spilled milk on the [   ].

(A)　　　　　　(B)　　　　　　(C)　　　　　　(D)

 Listen to the senctences and choose the best response.

1.

B: Can I see your new ⬚⬚⬚ ⬚⬚⬚ ?

G: _____.

(A) Sorry, I broke your ⬚⬚⬚ .

(B) ⬚⬚⬚ you do it until Friday.

(C) It's my pleasure. Ask me ⬚⬚⬚ .

(D) Sure, but be careful ⬚⬚⬚ it, please.

2.

M: You are driving ⬚⬚⬚ fast. You'll ⬚⬚⬚ a ticket.

W: _____.

(A) Be careful with the ⬚⬚⬚ water.

(B) Can you see the ⬚⬚⬚ on the floor?

(C) Don't be so ⬚⬚⬚ . I am just a little late.

(D) It's okay. Pay attention to speed ⬚⬚⬚ .

3.

B: This ⬚⬚⬚ stayed in the ⬚⬚⬚ for a week.

G: _____.

(A) If I were you, I wouldn't ⬚⬚⬚ .

(B) If I were you, I would ⬚⬚⬚ it now.

(C) If I were you, I wouldn't ⬚⬚⬚ that.

(D) If I were you, I would ⬚⬚⬚ it down.

UNIT 2 조언/충고

 Listen to the short talks or conversations and choose the best answer.

1.

> **B**: When you go ＿＿＿＿, pay attention to the ＿＿＿＿ of clothes.
>
> **G**: I'll ＿＿＿＿ to do that. But every store has a ＿＿＿＿ size.

What does the girl need to think about?

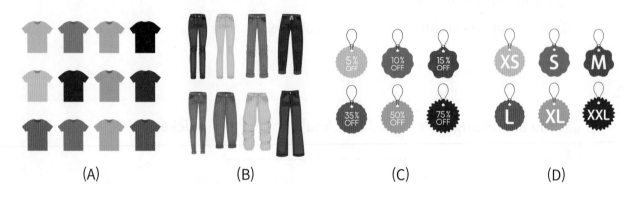

(A)　　　　　　(B)　　　　　　(C)　　　　　　(D)

2.

> **M**: My son loves ＿＿＿＿. I am worried ＿＿＿＿ his ＿＿＿＿.
>
> **W**: If I ＿＿＿＿ you, I wouldn't let him eat the ＿＿＿＿ thing.

What is the man's worry?

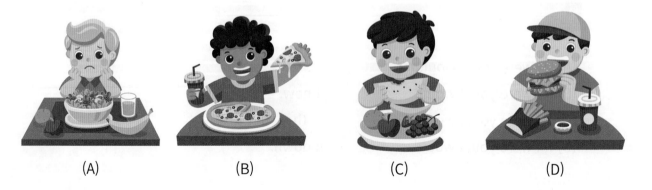

(A)　　　　　　(B)　　　　　　(C)　　　　　　(D)

 Listen to the conversations and choose the best response.

1.

> **B**: I'll give you a _____ . Give me the _____ .
>
> **G**: Thanks _____ be careful when you _____ it. It is _____ .
>
> **B**: Oh, it is! What is _____ it?

What's next?

(A) Thank you for your kindness.

(B) I have to send this to London.

(C) My mom put the thing inside it.

(D) There is a set of wine glasses.

2.

> **B**: Do you _____ ? The doctor told you to _____ .
>
> **G**: I _____ . Maybe I can _____ it tomorrow.
>
> **B**: You _____ pay _____ to the doctor's word!

What's next?

(A) Watch out for the tree.

(B) Alright, I'll go jogging now.

(C) I didn't understand the rules.

(D) Sounds great. Let's give it a try.

UNIT 2 조언/충고

Unit Review

Listen and complete the dialogue. Track 7-2-8

 What are some of the road _____ rules you know?

No crossing at a _____.

 You are _____. You _____ cross at a redlight.

No _____. You must cross _____ at crosswalks.

You should wear a _____ when you are on a bike.

 You are all correct!
Watch out for cars, _____ _____ to the lights
and be _____ when crossing the road.

Listen. Pause. Say each sentence.

Unit 03

규칙 / 금지

 What a mess! James, clean up your room and fold up your clothes now.

 Don't open your mouth when you eat your food.

Okay, mom.

 I am disappointed in you. I think you need to learn a lesson.

What lesson?

 No dessert for you today, James. Until you learn your manners, you must take out the trash too.

No way. That's not fair!

manners	예의	**fair**	공평한	**dessert**	디저트, 후식
learn	깨닫다, 깨우치다	**finish**	끝내다	**fold**	접다, 개키다
yell	소리 지르다	**quickly**	빨리, 빠르게	**until**	~까지
noise	소음	**nap**	낮잠	**study time**	공부 시간
game	경기, 시합	**disappointed**	실망한	**during**	~동안, ~중에

Before Practice

▶ Track 7-3-2

 토셀쌤의 Sound Tip

• 어려운 발음

noise
game

e

[E : 소리 없음]

단어가 [E]로 끝나는 경우,
대부분 발음하지 않는다.

tube

mate

kite

due

noise

Expressions. Listen and learn the expressions.

finish lunch
점심을 다 먹다

fold up clothes
옷을 접다

take out trash
쓰레기를 버리다

be disappointed
실망하다

 **Practice**

Step 1. Listen to the words and write.

❶

❻

❷

❼

❸

❽

❹

❾

❺

❿

Step 2. Listen to the dialogue and fill in the blanks.

❶ **M**: Can you _____ Jack our classroom _____ ?

G: No _____ on the phone in class and no _____ .

❷ **B**: I will _____ my homework after I take a nap.

G: You _____ sleep before _____ your homework.

Step 3. Complete the dialogue.

❶ **G**: I finished my lunch. Can I go to the soccer game now?

B: _____

❷ **G**: _____

B: You said we must stay quiet when studying.

 Listen to the sentences and choose the best picture.

1.

> **G**: No _____ on the _____ .

(A)   (B)   (C)   (D)

2.

> **B**: You should _____ your _____ _____ the table.

(A)   (B)   (C)   (D)

 Listen to the sentences and choose the best response.

1.

> **G**: What do you _____ about my new _____ ?
>
> **B**: _____ .

(A) You mustn't _____ in a restaurant.

(B) You must pay _____ at school.

(C) You must wear _____ when you go skiing.

(D) You mustn't wear _____ when you do sports.

2.

> **B**: Can I have a _____ of _____ now?
>
> **W**: _____ .

(A) Don't drink _____ at night.

(B) It's past 9 PM. No more _____ .

(C) She will eat _____ all day long.

(D) It's _____ 8 AM. I should hurry.

3.

> **B**: What did I say about good _____ _____ ?
>
> **G**: _____ .

(A) I shouldn't _____ around the table.

(B) I shouldn't _____ for others to start eating.

(C) I shouldn't _____ my mouth while eating.

(D) I shouldn't _____ my hands before eating.

 Listen to the short talks or conversations and choose the best answer.

1.

> B: Ah choo! Mom, I _____ I caught a _____ .
>
> W: From today, no _____ for you _____ you get _____ .

What is the food that the boy cannot eat from today?

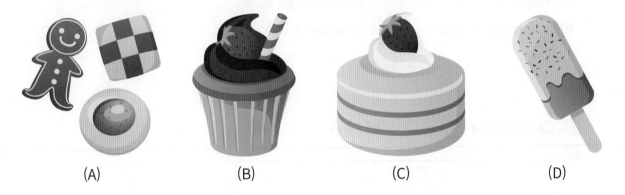

| (A) | (B) | (C) | (D) |

2.

> M: What did your _____ tell you about _____ manners?
>
> G: We must not _____ on the _____ inside the _____ .

What did the teacher say to the girl?

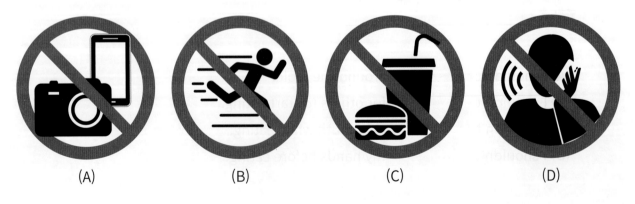

| (A) | (B) | (C) | (D) |

 Listen to the conversations and choose the best response.

1.

> B: Mom,   for   late.
>
> W: Why are you   in so late   ?
>
> B: In truth, Noah   me. He   my help.

What's next?

   (A) Hooray! You made it!

   (B) Super! You did a very good job.

   (C) Let's have a party to celebrate this.

   (D) No excuses. Now, no going out after 9.

2.

> B: This pen isn't   . You shouldn't   your friend's pen.
>
> G: It looked so   . So I   it in my bag.
>
> B: I am   in you. You should   it.

What's next?

   (A) No way. It's not fair.

   (B) This is my favorite pen.

   (C) Sorry, I'll give it back to her.

   (D) Hurry up! I am waiting outside.

Unit Review

Listen and complete the dialogue. Track 7-3-8

 What a _____!
James, clean up your room and _____ up your clothes now.

 _____ open your mouth when you eat your food.

Okay, mom.

 I am _____ in you.
I think you need to learn a _____.

What lesson?

No _____ for you today, James.
_____ you learn your manners,
you _____ take out the trash too.

No way. That's not _____!

 Listen. Pause. Say each sentence.

TOSEL 실전문제 ⑦

QR코드를 인식시키면
음원이 재생됩니다

1.

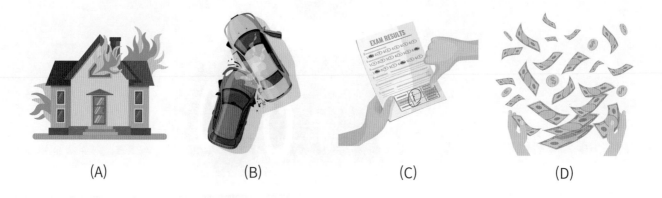

(A)　　　　　　　(B)　　　　　　　(C)　　　　　　　(D)

2.

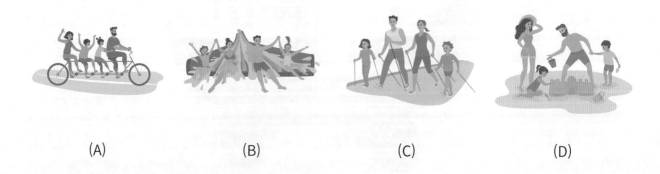

(A)　　　　　　　(B)　　　　　　　(C)　　　　　　　(D)

3.

(A)   (B)   (C)   (D)

4.

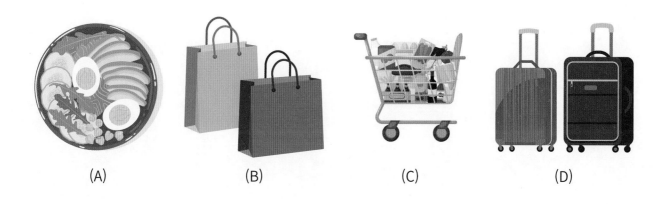

(A)   (B)   (C)   (D)

5.

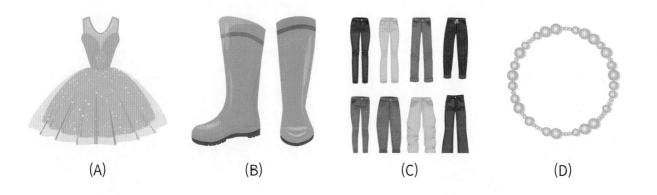

(A)   (B)   (C)   (D)

CHAPTER 08

Unit 01

주문 / 구매

 Let's go to the mall and buy some clothes.

That's great. We can have lunch there, too.

 Do you like this yellow dress?

No, I would like to get a red one instead. And, I'm starving.

 What would you like to order?

I'll get a chicken burger with extra cheese and fries, please.

I was so hungry from all that shopping.

 So how was today?

Awesome. I got new clothes and a delicious meal.

starving	굶주린	**instead**	대신에	**order**	주문하다
delicious	아주 맛있는	**meal**	식사	**laptop**	노트북
extra	추가의	**mall**	쇼핑 몰, 쇼핑 센터	**sale**	세일, 할인 판매
vegetarian	채식주의자	**beverage**	(물 외의) 음료	**electronic**	전자의
restaurant	식당, 레스토랑	**aisle**	통로	**device**	장치, 기기

토셀쌤의 Sound Tip

Before Practice

Track 8-1-2

• 어려운 발음

device / center

ce

① [ㅅ, ㅆ]: 단어 시작, 단어 끝에 [ce]가 있으면서, [a, e, i, o, r]과 가까이 있을 때
② [세, 쎄]: 가끔 단어 시작 위치에서 [세]나 [쎄]로 발음한다.

ice

peace

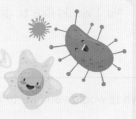
cell

celery

Expressions. Listen and learn the expressions.

on sale
할인을 하다

look for
~을 찾다

order something
~을 주문하다

electronic device
전자기기

Practice

 Track 8-1-3

Step 1. Listen to the words and write.

❶

❻

❷

❼

❸

❽

❹

❾

❺

❿

Step 2. Listen to the dialogue and fill in the blanks.

❶ G: Could you tell me _____ I can _____ the cookies, please?

M: You will find them on _____ six, beside the _____.

❷ G: If you need to get a new laptop, _____ _____ are on sale now.

B: _____ _____ is the new Samsung laptop?

Step 3. Complete the dialogue.

❶ B: Can I take your order?

G: _____

❷ R: _____

W: Here is a list of places selling vegetarian meals.

UNIT 1 주문/구매

Basic 215

 Listen to the sentences and choose the best picture.

1.

G : I _____ like meatball _____ with _____ sauce.

| (A) | (B) | (C) | (D) |

2.

B : Excuse me, I am _____ a _____ shirt.

| (A) | (B) | (C) | (D) |

Part B. Listen and Respond

Listen to the sentences and choose the best response.

1.

> B: What do you   on your   list?
>
> G: _____.

(A) It's on the   floor.

(B) When does the   close?

(C) Here is a list of people to   .

(D) I need some oranges and olive   .

2.

> B: Could you tell me   I can find a   store?
>
> G: _____.

(A) When does the store   ?

(B) It was my birthday   .

(C) I'll have this blue   .

(D) It's right   the toy store.

3.

> B: Can I   these shoes   ?
>
> W: _____.

(A) Of course. What size do you   ?

(B) Too small. Can I have a   size?

(C) I would like a   burger, please.

(D) You'll find them behind the   .

 Listen to the short talks or conversations and choose the best answer.

1.

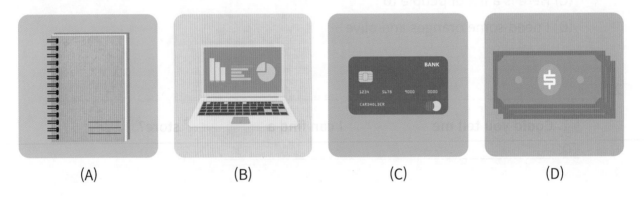

B: I'll _____ this christmas _____ and a yellow _____ .

W: Alright. How would you like to _____ ? _____ or credit card?

What is the boy buying?

(A)   (B)   (C)   (D)

2.

B: If you need to get _____ , _____ devices are on _____ now.

G: Thank you. Could you tell me _____ to find the _____ store?

Where does the girl need to go?

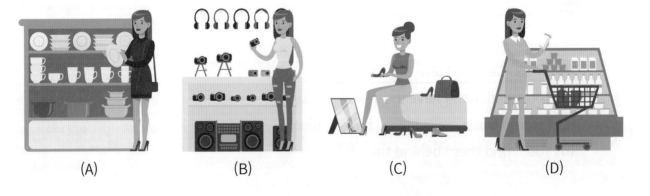

(A)   (B)   (C)   (D)

 Listen to the conversations and choose the best response.

1.

> M: These _____ are the most _____ ones here.
>
> G: I really like the _____. How much are _____?
>
> M: It is a _____ new _____. It's 68 dollars.

What's next?

    (A) Yes, I got it yesterday.

    (B) What is your shoe size?

    (C) Can I have some discount?

    (D) He took his shoes and socks off.

2.

> M: Do you _____ some _____?
>
> G: I am _____ for a vacuum _____.
>
> M: Oh, this _____ is on _____.

What's next?

    (A) Could I try this on?

    (B) Yes, that's a very good price.

    (C) Right, carrots are on the list.

    (D) No, you have to clean your room.

Unit Review

Listen and complete the dialogue. Track 8-1-8

 Let's go to the _____ and buy some clothes.

 That's great. We can have _____ there too.

 Do you like this _____ dress?

 No, I _____ like to get a red one instead. And, I'm _____.

 What would you like to _____?

 I'll _____ a chicken burger with _____ cheese and fries, please.

 I was so _____ from all that shopping.

 So _____ was today?

 Awesome. I got new clothes and a _____ meal.

🗣 Listen. Pause. Say each sentence.

Unit 02

위치 / 장소

 Excuse me, officer.
How do I get to the library from here?

This is where we are right now.
You have to walk straight passing three more blocks.

 I think I'm lost. Could you help me, please?
I'm looking for the library.

 Yes. You need to go one more block
and you will see a donut shop beside it.

 Thank you. Wish me luck!

Good luck on finding the library!

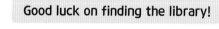

 Hey, that's the donut shop the lady mentioned.
I finally found it with kind help.

lost	길을 잃은	bank	은행	cross	건너다, 횡단하다
pass	지나가다	kind	친절한, 다정한	pharmacy	약국
block	(도로를 나뉘는) 구역, 블록	soccer field	축구장	light	신호등
donut	도넛	beside	옆에	take	
quickest	제일 빠른	aquarium	수족관	gas station	주유소

Before Practice

Track 8-2-2

 토셀쌤의 Sound Tip

- 어려운 발음

p̲h̲armacy

phone

dolphin

ph

[F]의 ['ㅍ]와 같은 발음이다.
윗니로 아랫입술을 지긋이 물고 발음한다.

trophy

graph

Expressions. Listen and learn the expressions.

walk straight
쭉 걸어가다

cross the street
길을 건너다

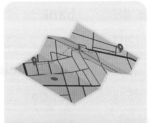

get somewhere
~에 도착하다

good luck on~
~에 행운을 빌다

 **Practice**

Step 1. Listen to the words and write.

❶

❷

❸

❹

❺

❻

❼

❽

❾

❿

Step 2. Listen to the dialogue and fill in the blanks.

❶ **B**: Do you know   the soccer   is?

G: the street and you will see it   the gas station.

❷ **B**: Excuse me, how do I get to the   from here?

G: Turn   at the next light, and it will be on your   .

Step 3. Complete the dialogue.

❶ **G**: What is the quickest way to get to the aquarium?

B:

❷ **G**:

B: Walk straight for 5 minutes, and you will find it.

 Listen to the sentences and choose the best picture.

1.

G: _____ you help me please? I'm looking for a _____ .

(A)

(B)

(C)

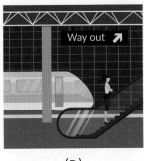
(D)

2.

B: Excuse me, do you know where _____ is?

(A)

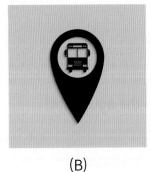
(B)

(C)

(D)

 Listen to the sentences and choose the best response.

1.

> B : Pardon me. Is there a   here?
>
> G : _____.

(A) It is just around the   .

(B)   all the electric devices.

(C) There is a shop under the   .

(D) We   the hill to the house.

2.

> B : Can you tell me the   way to get   Seoul?
>
> G : _____.

(A) I study best in the   .

(B) Taking the   is the best.

(C) They walked   the park.

(D) We will   at the next stop.

3.

> B : Do you know   the National   is?
>
> G : _____.

(A) Our house is   the sea.

(B) The   opens at 10 AM.

(C) Let's go for a walk   the river.

(D) Go straight two   and turn left.

UNIT 2 위치 / 장소

 Listen to the short talks or conversations and choose the best answer.

1.

B: Can you help me _____? I am _____ this place.

G: Go straight one _____ and turn right. It's _____ a cinema.

Where is the boy trying to go?

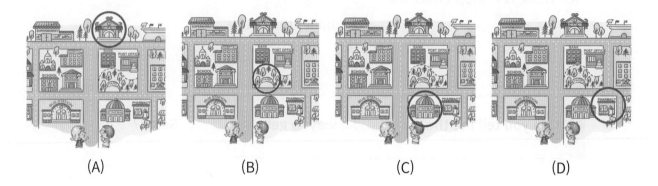

(A)   (B)   (C)   (D)

2.

B: Excuse me, how do I get to Incheon _____ from _____?

G: The _____ way to get there is by taking the _____.

How will the boy get to Incheon Airport?

(A)   (B)   (C)   (D)

 Listen to the conversations and choose the best response.

1.

> **B** : I think we are going to _____ our _____ .
>
> **G** : Sorry, I had to bring my _____ . I _____ it at home.
>
> **B** : Let's hurry. What is the _____ way to get to the _____ ?

What's next?

  (A) Let's take a taxi.

  (B) Let's go to the aquarium.

  (C) I get off at the next station.

  (D) The subway is very crowded.

2.

> **B** : _____ . How do I get to the opera house?
>
> **G** : It's not _____ from here. Do you see the _____ ?
>
> **B** : Yes, I see it _____ a hotel.

What's next?

  (A) I didn't really like the opera.

  (B) Can you find a hotel for me?

  (C) You can go to the opera house by bus.

  (D) The opera house is opposite the hotel.

Unit Review

Listen and complete the dialogue.  Track 8-2-8

 Excuse me, officer.
How do I get to the _____ from here?

You have to walk _____ This is where we are right now.
You have to walk _____ passing three more blocks.

 I think I'm _____. Could you help me please?
I'm _____ _____ the library.

Yes. You _____ to go one more block
and you will see a donut shop _____ it.

 Thank you. _____ me luck!

Good _____ on finding the library!

 Hey, that's the donut shop the lady _____.
I finally _____ it with _____ help.

 Listen. Pause. Say each sentence.

Unit 03

사건 / 상황

 Something big happened yesterday while I was at the library.

What happened?

 I was studying for a test and suddenly the fire alarm went off.

 I thought it was a fire drill. So I went out of the building.

But when I got out, I found out that the library was really on fire!

It's a good thing that you escaped on time.

suddenly	갑자기	**drill** (비상시를 대비한) 훈련		**parade**	퍼레이드
alarm	경보기	**cotton candy**	솜사탕	**festival**	축제
escape	탈출하다	**cotton**	솜	**university**	대학교
neighbor	이웃	**happen**	발생하다	**noise**	소음
tasty	맛있는	**while**	~동안	**sleepy**	졸린

Before Practice

Track 8-3-2

 토셀쌤의 Sound Tip

• 어려운 발음

cotton

-t 모음 n

[콭]까지 발음하고
혀가 입 천장에 붙었을 때,
혀를 입 천장으로 한번 더 꾹 눌러주며
발음한다.

button

rotten

eaten

mountain

cotton

Expressions. Listen and learn the expressions.

set something on fire
불을 지르다

go off
~가 울리다

fight over
~때문에 싸우다

on time
시간 맞춰서

Step 1. Listen to the words and write.

❶

❻

❷

❼

❸

❽

❹

❾

❺

❿

Step 2. Listen to the dialogue and fill in the blanks.

❶ **G**: Did you _____ that there was a _____ at the _____ ?

B: Yes, I heard that someone _____ the university on _____ .

❷ **G**: Did you go to the _____ during the weekend?

B: Yes, I ate _____ candy and _____ the _____ .

Step 3. Complete the dialogue.

❶ **G**: _____

B: The boys are fighting over a toy robot.

❷ **G**: You look sleepy. _____

B: I couldn't sleep because my neighbor made a lot of noise.

 Listen to the sentences and choose the best picture.

1.

> B : There was an _____ on the _____ .

(A)

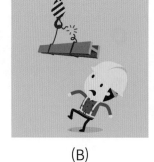
(B)

(C)

(D)

2.

> G : I heard someone _____ Mia's _____ .

(A)

(B)

(C)

(D)

✏️ **Listen to the sentences and choose the best response.**

1.

> B: What ▢▢▢▢▢ ▢▢▢▢▢ your leg?
>
> G: _____.

    (A) Don't run too ▢▢▢▢▢ .

    (B) I went to bed ▢▢▢▢▢ .

    (C) I ▢▢▢▢▢ the stairs.

    (D) I can ▢▢▢▢▢ one leg.

2.

> B: I heard a man ▢▢▢▢▢ to the ▢▢▢▢▢ .
>
> G: _____.

    (A) What is ▢▢▢▢▢ on?

    (B) What is the ▢▢▢▢▢ ?

    (C) What ▢▢▢▢▢ you doing?

    (D) What's ▢▢▢▢▢ with you?

3.

> B: The ▢▢▢▢▢ is ▢▢▢▢▢ .
>
> G: _____.

    (A) Where did you ▢▢▢▢▢ ?

    (B) How did that ▢▢▢▢▢ ?

    (C) Did you ▢▢▢▢▢ a nice time?

    (D) Does she come here ▢▢▢▢▢ ?

Listen to the short talks or conversations and choose the best answer.

1.

B : They don't talk to each other. What happened _____ them?

G : They had a big _____ over _____ .

What happened between them?

| (A) | (B) | (C) | (D) |

2.

G : Did you hear that Lucy _____ her _____ this week?

B : She _____ be really sad. I had the same experience with my dog.

What did Lucy lose?

| (A) | (B) | (C) | (D) |

Part D. **Listen and Speak**

 Listen to the conversations and choose the best response.

1.

> **B**: What's   here?
> **G**: Do you know   about   ?
> **B**: Not really. Please   where we are.

What's next?

(A) We usually go by car.

(B) He came last in the race.

(C) We are inside the racetrack.

(D) He camped overnight in a field.

2.

> **B**: Did you hear   Barbara was   by a car?
> **G**: Oh, no.   did the accident   ?
> **B**: She   across the   .

What's next?

A) I didn't see her there.

(B) I saw my doctor today.

(C) We just crossed the road.

(D) I hope she gets well soon.

Unit Review

Listen and complete the dialogue.

▶ Track 8-3-8

Something _____ happened yesterday _____ I was at the library.

What _____?

I was _____ for a test and suddenly the fire alarm went _____.

FIRE ALARM

I thought it was a fire _____. So I went _____ of the building.

_____ when I got out, I found out that the library was really on _____!

It's a good thing that you _____ on time.

 Listen. Pause. Say each sentence.

TOSEL 실전문제 ⑧

QR코드를 인식시키면
음원이 재생됩니다

SECTION I. Listening and Speaking

In SECTION I, you will be asked to demonstrate how well you understand spoken English. You will have approximately 5 minutes to complete this section.

SECTION I은 듣기 능력을 평가합니다.

PART A. Listen and Recognize

DIRECTIONS: For questions 1 to 5, listen to the sentences and choose the BEST picture. The sentences will be spoken **TWICE.**

지시 사항: 1번부터 5번까지는 문장을 듣고, 가장 알맞은 그림을 고르는 문제입니다.
문제는 **두 번씩** 들려줍니다.

1.

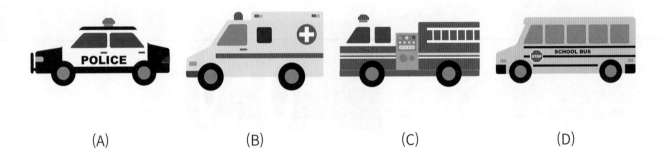

(A)   (B)   (C)   (D)

2.

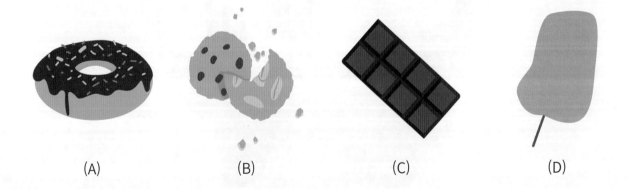

(A)   (B)   (C)   (D)

3.

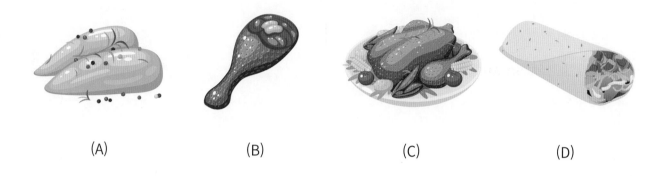

(A)   (B)   (C)   (D)

4.

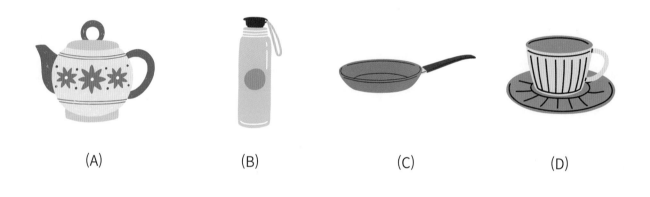

(A)   (B)   (C)   (D)

5.

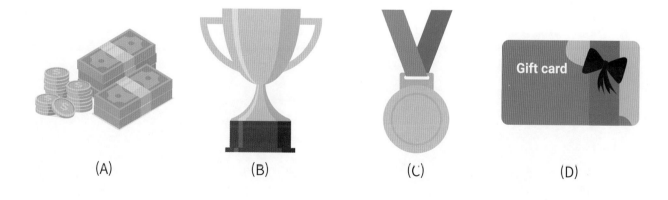

(A)   (B)   (C)   (D)

Appendix

A

AM	addr. 오전
abroad	adv. 해외로
action	n. 행동
after	prep. ~뒤에, 후에
agree	v. 동의하다, 찬성하다
aisle	n. 통로
alarm	n. 경보기
allow	v. 용납하다
alright	adj. 괜찮은, 무사한
also	adv. 또한
amazing	adj. 멋진, 훌륭한
amusement park	n. 놀이공원
annoyed	adj. 짜증이 난
another	pron. 또 하나의, 다른
answer	n. 답, 정답
anymore	adv. 더이상
anything	pron. 무엇이든
aquarium	n. 수족관
around	adv. 약, 쯤, 주위에
as a child	adv. 어릴 때
assignment	n. 과세
at all	adv. 전혀, 조금도
attention	n. 주의
autograph	n. (유명인의) 사인

B

bad	adj. 나쁜, 미안한
ballpark	n. 야구장
bandage	n. 붕대
bank	n. 은행
bark	v. 짖다
because	conj. ~때문에
bedroom	n. 침실
before	prep. ~전에, 앞에
behind	prep. ~뒤에, 뒤떨어져
believe	v. 믿다
beneath	prep. 아래에
beside	prep. 옆에
better	adv. 더 좋은, 나은
beverage	n. (물 외의) 음료
bike	n. 자전거
bin	n. 쓰레기통
birthday	n. 생일
block	n. (도로를 나뉘는) 구역, 블록
book	v. 예약하다
bread	n. 빵

break	v. 부서지다		cotton	n. 솜
brick	n. 벽돌		cotton candy	n. 솜사탕
bright	adj. 밝은		cross	v. 건너다, 횡단하다
bring	v. 가져오다		crosswalk	n. 횡단보도
buy	v. 사다		culture	n. 문화
by myself	adv. 스스로		**D**	
C			daily	adv. 매일
calm	adj. 차분한, 침착한		delicious	adj. 아주 맛있는
careful	adj. 조심하는		describe	v. 묘사하다
carry	v. 운반하다		dessert	n. 디저트, 후식
castle	n. 성		device	n. 장치, 기기
chat	v. 수다를 떨다		dirty	adj. 더러운
check	v. 확인하다		disagree	v. 반대하다
cheer up	phr. 힘 내, 기운 내		disappointed	adj. 실망한
chores	n. 집안일		dish	n. 접시
Christmas	n. 크리스마스		donut	n. 도넛
classmate	n. 반 친구		downtown	n. 번화가
classroom	n. 교실		drill	n. (비상시를 대비한) 훈련
congrats	n. / phr. 축하, 축하해!		due	adj. ~할 예정인, 예정된
congratulations	n. / phr. 축하, 축하해요!		during	prep. ~동안, ~중에
copy	v. 베끼다		**E**	
cost	v. 비용이 들다		early	adv. 이른, 빠른
costume	n. 의상		electronic	adj. 전자의

end	n. 끝; v. 끝나다		file	n. 파일, 서류파일
enjoy	v. 즐기다		final exam	n. 기말 시험
enough	adv. 충분한		finally	adv. 마침내, 마지막으로
escape	v. 탈출하다		finish	v. 끝내다
every	adj. 모든, 매		fix	v. 고치다
every day	adv. 매일		floor	n. 바닥
everything	pron. 모든 것		fly	v. 비행하다, 비행기를 타다
everywhere	adv. 모든 곳에서		fold	v. 접다, 개키다
exam	n. 시험		follow	v. 따라가다, 따르다
excellent	adj. 훌륭한		footprint	n. 발자국
exciting	adj. 신나는, 흥미진진한		forget	v. 잊어버리다
exercise	v. 운동하다		free time	n. 자유 시간
exhausted	adj. 지친		friendly	adj. 친절한, 다정한
experience	n. 경험		full	adv. 가득한
extra	adj. 여분의, 추가의		**G**	
F			game	n. 경기, 시합
fair	adj. 공평한		garbage	n. 쓰레기
fairy tale	n. 동화		gas station	n. 주유소
fall	v. 넘어지다		get	v. 받다, 얻다
favorite	adj. 가장 좋아하는		ghost	n. 귀신
festival	n. 축제		give back	v. 돌려주다
field trip	n. 현장학습, 견학		glad	adj. 기쁜, 기꺼이 ~하려는
fight	n. 싸움; v. 싸우다		grass	n. 풀, 잔디

groceries	n. 슈퍼마켓

H

half	n. 절반
hallway	n. 복도
hand	n. 도움
handle	v. 다루다, 처리하다
happen	v. 발생하다, 일어나다
hate	v. 몹시 싫어하다
have	v. 먹다
have to	modal. ~해야 하다
heavy	adj. 무거운
helmet	n. 헬멧
holiday	n. 휴가, 연휴
honest	adj. 솔직한
hope	v. 바라다, 희망하다
hospital	n. 병원

I

idea	n. 아이디어
instead	adv. 대신에
instruction	n. 지시
introduce	v. 소개하다
invite	v. 초대하다

J

jaywalking	n. 무단 횡단
jog	v. 조깅하다
joy	n. 기쁨, 즐거움
jump	v. 점프하다

K

kind	adj. 친절한, 다정한
knee	n. 무릎

L

language	n. 언어
laptop	n. 휴대용 컴퓨터
learn	v. 깨닫다, 깨우치다
leave	v. 남기다
lend	v. 빌려주다
library	n. 도서관
light	n. 신호등
little	adj. 작은
long face	n. 시무룩한 얼굴
look for	v. 찾다
lost	adj. 길을 잃은
lottery	n. 복권

M

mad	adj. 화가 난

make it	성공하다	nothing	pron. 아무것도
mall	n. 쇼핑 몰, 쇼핑 센터	**O**	
manners	n. 예의	offer	n. 제의
meal	n. 식사	often	adv. 자주, 흔히
mess	n. 엉망	on my own	스스로
mind	n. 마음, 정신	once	adv. 한 번
miss	v. 놓치다	once a week	adv. 일주일에 한 번
mistake	n. 실수	opinion	n. 의견
monster	n. 괴물	order	v. 주문하다
month	n. 달, 월	own	adj. 자신의, 직접 ~한
N		**P**	
nap	n. 낮잠	PM	abbr. 오후
nature	n. 자연	parade	n. 퍼레이드
need	v. 필요하다	parents	n. 부모
neighbor	n. 이웃	pass	v. 지나가다
never	adv. 결코 ~않다	pasta	n. 파스타
New Year's Day	phr. 새해 첫 날	perfect	adj. 완벽한
next	adj. 다음	personally	adv. 개인적으로
next time	phr. 다음에	pharmacy	n. 약국
no problem	phr. 문제 없다, 괜찮다	photocopy	v. 복사하다
no way	phr. 말도 안돼!	picnic	n. 소풍
noise	n. 소음	picture	n. 사진
normally	adv. 보통, 정상적으로	place	n. 장소

plan	n. 계획		right away	adv. 곧바로, 즉시
plenty	adv. 충분히		road	n. 도로
pollution	n. 오염		rocking horse	n. 흔들 목마
power	n. 힘		roller coaster	n. 롤러코스터
practice	v. 연습하다		roommate	n. 룸메이트
present	n. 선물		routine	n. 일상
prize	n. 상		rule	n. 규칙
problem	n. 문제		**S**	
promise	n. 약속		safe	adj. 안전한
Q			safety	n. 안전
quickest	adj. 제일 빠른		sale	n. 세일, 할인 판매
quickly	adv. 빨리, 빠르게		salty	adj. 소금이 든, 짭짤한
quiet	adj. 조용한		save	v. 구하다, 절약하다
R			scary	adj. 무서운
real	adj. 실제의		schedule	n. 계획, 스케줄
really	adv. 실제로, 정말로		school uniform	n. 교복
reduce	v. 줄이다		score	n. 점수
reflect on	v. 반성하다		season	n. 계절
relax	v. 휴식하다		send	v. 보내다
responsible	adj. 책임이 있는		serious	adj. 진지한
rest	n. 휴식		share	v. 나누다, 공유하다
restaurant	n. 식당, 레스토랑		should	modal. ~해야 한다
ride	v. 타다		skill	n. 기량, 기술

sleepy	adj. 졸리운, 졸음이 오는		superhero	n. 슈퍼히어로
slip	v. 미끄러지다		surprise	v. 놀라움
soccer field	n. 축구장		**T**	
sometimes	adv. 때때로, 가끔		take	v. (교통수단 등을) 타다, (얼마의 시간이) 걸리다
soon	adv. 곧		tasty	adj. 맛있는
sound	v. ~인 것 같다		teammate	n. 팀 동료
souvenir	n. 기념품		temple stay	n. 템플스테이
speech	n. 연설, 강의		text	n. 문자 메시지
spend	v. (시간을) 보내다		theater	n. 극장
sports day	n. 운동회		thrilled	adj. 신이 난
stain	n. 얼룩		throw	v. (파티를)벌이다, 열다
stand	v. 서 있다		ticket	n. 표, 티켓
starving	adj. 굶주린		tired	adj. 피곤한
stay	v. (상태를) 유지하다, 머물다		tomorrow	n. 내일
still	adv. 여전히		toy	n. 장난감
strict	adj. 엄격한		trash	n. 쓰레기
strongly	adv. 강하게		travel	v. 여행하다
study abroad	v. 유학하다		tray	n. 쟁반
study time	n. 공부시간		true	adj. 사실인, 진짜의
suddenly	adv. 갑자기		truth	n. 사실
suggestion	n. 제안		truthfully	adv. 진실하게
summer	n. 어름		try	v. 시도해보다
sunny	adj. 화창한		twice	adv. 두 번, 두 배로

U

university	n. 대학교
until	conj. ~까지
upset	adj. 화난
usually	adv. 보통, 대개

V

vacation	n. 방학, 휴가
vegetarian	n. 채식주의자
visit	v. 방문하다
volleyball	n. 배구
vote	v. 투표하다

W

wake-up call	n. 모닝콜
wash	v. 씻다
wear	v. 착용하다
wedding	n. 결혼
week	n. 주
weekend	n. 주말
weekly	adj. 매주의
welcome	v. 환영하다
well	adj. 좋은, 건강한
while	conj. ~동안, ~중에
win	v. 이기다

windy	adj. 바람이 많이 부는
wish	v, n. 원하다, 바라다, 소망
wonderful	adj. 아주 멋진, 훌륭한
woof	int. 개가 크게 짖는 소리
worry	v. 걱정하다

Y

year	n. 년, 해
yearly	adj. 매년
yell	v. 소리 지르다
younger	adj. 더 어린

엄선된 **100만 명**의 응시자 성적 데이터를 활용한 **AI기반** 데이터 공유 및 가치 고도화 **플랫폼**

TOSEL® Lab

공동기획
- 고려대학교 문과대학 언어정보연구소
- 국제토셀위원회

TOSEL Lab 이란?

국내외 15,000여 개 학교·학원 단체응시인원 중 엄선한 100만 명 이상의 실제 TOSEL 성적 데이터와, 정부(과학기술정보통신부)의 AI 바우처 지원 사업 수행기관 선정으로 개발된 맞춤식 AI 빅데이터 기반 영어성장 플랫폼입니다.

TOSEL Lab
지정교육기관 혜택

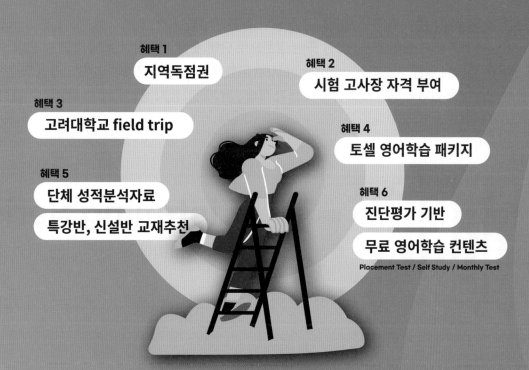

혜택 1
지역독점권

혜택 2
시험 고사장 자격 부여

혜택 3
고려대학교 field trip

혜택 4
토셀 영어학습 패키지

혜택 5
단체 성적분석자료

특강반, 신설반 교재추천

혜택 6
진단평가 기반

무료 영어학습 컨텐츠

Placement Test / Self Study / Monthly Test

학원장의 실질적인 비용부담 없이
TOSEL® Lab
브랜드를 사용할 수 있는 기회

TOSEL Lab 에는 어떤 콘텐츠가 있나요?

진단
맞춤형 레벨테스트로
정확한 평가 제공

> 응시자 빅데이터 분석에 기반한
> 테스트로 신규 상담 학생의
> 영어능력을 정확하게 진단하고
> 효과적인 영어 교육을 실시하기
> 위한 객관적인 가이드라인을
> 제공합니다.

교재
세분화된 레벨로
실력에 맞는 학습 제공

> TOSEL의 세분화된 교재 레벨은
> 각 연령에 맞는 어휘와 읽기
> 지능 및 교과 과정과의 연계가
> 가능하도록 설계된 교재들로
> 효과적인 학습 커리큘럼을
> 제공합니다.

학습
다양한 교재연계 콘텐츠로
효과적인 자기주도학습

> TOSEL 시험을 대비한 다양한
> 콘텐츠를 제공해 영어 학습에
> 시너지 효과를 기대할 수
> 있으며, 학생들의 자기주도
> 학습 습관을 더 탄탄하게
> 키울 수 있습니다.

Reading Series
내신과 토셀 고득점을 한꺼번에

Pre-Starter Starter Basic Junior High-Junior

- 각 단원 학습 도입부에 주제와 관련된 이미지를 통한 말하기 연습
- 각 Unit 별 4-6개의 목표 단어 제시, 그림 또는 영문으로 단어 뜻을 제공하여 독해 학습 전 단어 숙지
- 독해&실용문 연습을 위한 지문과 Comprehension 문항을 10개씩 수록하여 이해도 확인 및 진단
- 숙지한 독해 지문을 원어민 음성으로 들으며 듣기 학습 , 듣기 전, 듣기 중, 듣기 후 학습 커리큘럼 마련

Listening Series
한국 학생들에게 최적화된 듣기 실력 완성!

Pre-Starter Starter Basic Junior High-Junior

- 초등 / 중등 교과과정 연계 말하기&듣기 학습과 세분화된 레벨
- TOSEL 기출 문장과 실생활에 자주 활용되는 문장 패턴을 통해 듣기 및 말하기 학습
- 실제 TOSEL 지문의 예문을 활용한 실용적 학습 제공
- 실전 감각 향상과 점검을 위한 기출 문제 수록

Speaking Serie
출간예정

Grammar Series

체계적인 단계별 **문법 지침서**

Pre-Starter | Starter | Basic | Junior | High-Junior

- 초등 / 중등 교과과정 연계 문법 학습과 세분화된 레벨
- TOSEL 기출 문제 연습과 최신 수능 출제 문법을 포함하여 수능 / 내신 대비 가능
- 이해하기 쉬운 그림, 깔끔하게 정리된 표와 설명, 다양한 문제를 통해 문법 학습
- 실전 감각 향상과 점검을 위한 기출 문제 수록

Voca Series

학년별 꼭 알아야하는 **단어 수록!**

Pre-Starter | Starter | Basic | Junior | High-Junior

- 각 단어 학습 도입부에 주제와 관련된 이미지를 통한 말하기 연습
- TOSEL 시험을 기준으로 빈출 지표를 활용한 예문과 문제 구성
- 실제 TOSEL 지문의 예문을 활용한 실용적 학습 제공
- 실전 감각 향상과 점검을 위한 실전 문제 수록

Story Series

읽는 재미에 실력까지 **동시에!**

Pre-Starter | Starter | Basic | Junior

- 초등 / 중등 교과과정 연계 영어 학습과 세분화된 레벨
- 이야기 지문과 단어를 함께 연결지어 학생들의 독해 능력을 평가
- 이해하기 쉬운 그림, 깔끔하게 정리된 표와 설명, 다양한 문제, 재미있는 스토리를 통한 독해 학습
- 다양한 단계의 문항을 풀어보고 학생들의 읽기, 듣기, 쓰기, 말하기 실력을 집중적으로 향상

교재를 100% 활용하는 TOSEL Lab 지정교육기관의 노하우!

Teaching Materials

TOSEL에서 제공하는 수업 자료로
교재 학습을 더욱 효과적으로 진행!

Study Content

철저한 자기주도학습 콘텐츠로
교재 수업 후 효과적인 복습!

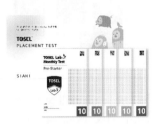

Test Content

교재 학습과 더불어 학생 맞춤형
시험으로 실력 점검 및 향상

100만 명으로 엄선된 **TOSEL**
성적 데이터로 탄생!

TOSEL Lab 지정교육기관을 위한 콘텐츠로 더욱 효과적인 수업을 경험하세요.

국제토셀위원회는 TOSEL Lab 지정교육기관에서 교재로
수업하는 학원을 위해 교재를 잘 활용할 수 있는 다양한
콘텐츠를 제공 및 지원합니다.

TOSEL Lab 지정교육기관은

국제토셀위원회 직속 TOSEL연구소에서 20년 동안 보유해온
전국 15,000여 개 교육기관 토셀 응시자들의 영어성적 분석데이터를
공유받아, 통계를 기반으로 한 전문적이고 과학적인 커리큘럼을 설계하고,
영어학습 방향을 제시하여, 경쟁력있는 기관, 잘 가르치는 기관으로
해당 지역에서 입지를 다지게 됩니다.

TOSEL Lab 지정교육기관으로 선정되기 위해서는
소정의 **심사 절차**가 수반됩니다.

TOSEL Lab
심사신청

TOSEL Lab
더 알아보기

TOSEL° Lab 🌿

Answers

Short Answers

UNIT 1
Practice
p.19

1. (1) neighbor (2) grade (3) pleased (4) major (5) get together (6) introduce (7) pretty (8) call (9) myself (10) often

2. (1) How, doing, doing, good, How, about   (2) introduce, myself, new, major, studying, too, get, together

3. (1) I'm in the third grade.   (2) Pleased to meet you. I'm Jack.

Part A
p.20

1. (A), saying, neighbor

2. (C), major, science

Part B
p.21

1. (D), What grade, student, am from, am afraid of, sixth grade

2. (D), neighbors, moved, look, went, work, Let's

3. (A), How, doing, Pretty, later, Have, meet

Part C
p.22

1. (B), heavy, need, moved in

2. (C), major, history, majoring, in

Part D
p.23

1. (B), have, student, everyone, tell, us, yourself

2. (C), Welcome, High, first, day, How, doing

UNIT 2
Practice
p.27

1. (1) introduce (2) parent (3) little (4) favorite (5) picnic (6) friendly (7) enjoy (8) share (9) bring (10) fairy tale

2. (1) introduce, enjoy, fairy tale   (2) share, playing

3. (1) She works in a bank.   (2) Today, I brought my cat with me.

Part A
p.28

1. (B), works, restaurant

2. (C), tells, stories

Part B
p.29

1. (A), share, past, wait, happened, boring, What

2. (C), What, food, ate, Chinese, enjoy, brought

3. (C), talk about, favorate, loud, work, listening, myself

Part C
p.30

1. (B), this, my, high, pleasure, meet

2. (B), introduce, favorite, eyes, brown

Part D
p.31

1. (D), name, manager, Nice, meet, please, meet

2. (C), please, say, so, cute, my, boy

UNIT 3
Practice
p.35

1. (1) beside (2) describe (3) bedroom (4) behind (5) full (6) in front of (7) bring (8) grass (9) castle (10) beneath

2. (1) describe, beneath   (2) standing, in front of, behind

3. (1) They are sitting side by side on the chair.   (2) He is lying down on the grass with his dog.

Part A
p.36

1. (B), raising, hands

2. (C), blue, clock

Part B
p.37

1. (D), What, doing, on, writing, eating, standing

2. (A), beside, mine, are, watching, hand

3. (D), long, behind, thank you, Did, jacket, bought

Part C
p.38

1. (B), and, are, lying, know, owner

2. (A), Can, describe, me, are, books, read

Part D
p.39

1. (D), so, late, hurry, catch, Where, is

2. (C), How, doing, brought, share with, Where, picture

TOSEL 실전문제 1   1. (A)   2. (B)   3. (B)   4. (D)   5. (C)

UNIT 1
Practice
p.47

1. (1) early (2) before (3) chat (4) sometimes (5) usually (6) once (7) normally (8) often (9) never (10) downtown

2. (1) What time, usually, Around, every   (2) how, spend, free time, hanging out, on

3. (1) How do you go to school?   (2) How often do you dance?

Part A
p.48

1. (B), swimming, every

2. (A), usually, washes, breakfast

Part B
p.49

1. (D), get, work, brushing, left, around, before

2. (B), Does, night, every, never, didn't, taking

3. (D), often, messages, little, nothing, by, week

Part C
p.50

1. (B), How, go, take, bus

2. (C), often, amusement park, normally, once, month

Part D
p.51

1. (C), came, meet, not, right, where, find

2. (A), spend, afternoon, sometimes, reading, at, home

UNIT 2
Practice
p.55

1. (1) season (2) skill (3) half (4) month (5) should (6) because (7) windy (8) favorite (9) take (10) around

2. (1) weather, today, windy, forget, jacket   (2) time, come, house, Around, 7, taking, bus

3. (1) My favorite season is winter because I can play in the snow.   (2) How long did it take to pick up that skill?

Part A
p.56

1. (B), sunscreen, cloudy

2. (C), takes, hours

Part B
p.57

1. (C), weather, like, Thursday, half, cold, fire

2. (C), What, late, will, July, only, storm

3. (B), How long, big, days, place, takes

Part C
p.58

1. (B), Why, raincoat, it, rain

2. (A), favorite, season, winter, in front of

Part D
p.59

1. (D), How, look, snow, afternoon, should, wear

2. (C), look, up, finished, reading, did, take

UNIT 3
Practice
p.63

1. (1) spend (2) train (3) sleepy (4) rest (5) excellent (6) no way (7) tired (8) calm (9) annoyed (10) until

2. (1) practiced, exhausted, Until, get, rest   (2) annoyed, calm, calm, give, back

3. (1) Why do you look so tired?   (2) I am so sleepy now, but tomorrow is the exam.

Part A
p.64

1. (C), tired, hungry

2. (B), annoyed, with, students

Part B
p.65

1. (C), close, window, little, open, cold, out

2. (B), gave, presentation, quiet, brave, difficult, good

3. (D), feel, well, How, Where, midnight, should

Part C
p.66

1. (B), spend, time, pool, get, some, rest

2. (A), hiking, weekend, mountain, me, dizzy

Part D
p.67

1. (D), What, matter, tired of, fighting, never, stays

2. (C), Here, medicine, How much, feel, sleepy

TOSEL 실전문제 2   1. (C)   2. (A)   3. (D)   4. (B)   5. (C)

UNIT 1
Practice
p.75

1. (1) amazing   (2) excited   (3) thrilled   (4) joy   (5) ride   (6) travel   (7) left   (8) idea   (9) classmate   (10) another

2. (1) can't, wait, house, excited   (2) new

3. (1) I'm thrilled that we can ride a roller coaster this time!   (2) Is the news about traveling to another country?

Part A
p.76

1. (D), looking, opening, hair

2. (A), thrilled, bake, cookies

Part B
p.77

1. (A), Did, bicycle, jumped, cried, stop, takes

2. (D), hear, won, hear, wait, mood, news

3. (D), got, letter, matter, lost, letter, amazing

Part C
p.78

1. (B), present, use, exercise, jump rope, needed

2. (A), wallet, left, car, wallet, made

Part D
p.79

1. (D), Did, good, yet, about, won, prize, contest

2. (C), Are, concert, booked, ticket, excited, autograph

UNIT 2
Practice
p.83

1. (1) win   (2) birthday   (3) wish   (4) really   (5) hope   (6) wish list   (7) lottery   (8) Christmas   (9) true   (10) share

2. (1) hope, get, Christmas, hope, book   (2) wish, make, wished, new

3. (1) I really hope that we will pass the final exam.   (2) I wished I would win the lottery.

Part A
p.84

1. (B), Christmas gift, necklace

2. (A), baker

Part B
p.85

1. (B), wish, luck, What, birthday, job

2. (D), hope for, Tell me, story book, everything, war

3. (C), live in, like, Where, true, happening

Part C
p.86

1. (B), lost, airport, finds

2. (C), Spain, next year

Part D
p.87

1. (D), magic lamp, wishes, first, family, second

2. (B), yesterday, game, rain, weather

UNIT 3
Practice
p.91

1. (1) fall   (2) salty   (3) problem   (4) enough   (5) stain   (6) fix   (7) hospital   (8) long   (9) check out   (10) fight

2. (1) problem, clothes, angry, stain, dress   (2) long, face, fought, friend

3. (1) Excuse me but this pasta is very salty.   (2) I don't feel well today. I am going to the hospital.

Part A
p.92

1. (A), fight, noisy

2. (D), down, failed, exam

Part B
p.93

1. (B), feel, well, hospital, get well, enough, Where

2. (C), steak, enough, deal, salty, back, expensive

3. (C), will, late, doing, feelings, take, mood

Part C
p.94

1. (B), What, wrong, so, have, soup

2. (A), problem, with, bought, these, too

Part D
p.95

1. (B), Excuse, not, happy, wrong, with, broken

2. (D), look, down, broke, with, anything, help

TOSEL 실전문제 3   1. (A)   2. (B)   3. (D)   4. (A)   5. (C)

UNIT 1		1. (1) prize (2) mistake (3) wedding (4) wonderful (5) speech (6) practice (7) congra-tulation (8) score (9) finally (10) make

UNIT 1

1. (1) prize　(2) mistake　(3) wedding　(4) wonderful　(5) speech　(6) practice　(7) congra-tulation　(8) score　(9) finally　(10) make

2. (1) Contratulations, won, first, made, Thank you, believe　(2) perfect, score, good, job

3. (1) congrats on your wedding! You're wonderful!　(2) It was great! You did it really well.

1. (B), did, planning, wedding

2. (A), Congrats, Wishing, house

1. (B), got, project, luck, for, wishes, thanks

2. (D), first, congrats, job, Good, yourself, much

3. (C), hear, won, hard, birthday, made it, lose

1. (D), news, had, baby, Congratulations, new

2. (C), on, graduation, still, believe, myself

1. (B), perfect, contest, done, difficult, made, mistake

2. (C), How, do, came, third, might, down

UNIT 2

1. (1) vote　(2) nature　(3) aquarium　(4) opinion　(5) save　(6) better　(7) think　(8) field trip　(9) disagree　(10) agree

2. (1) field trip, cold, think, go, temple　(2) think, movie, about, beauty, agree, power

3. (1) I disagree with you because buying a school uniform costs a lot of money.　(2) I strongly agree with you. And we can save nature by doing that.

1. (A), believe, salt, health

2. (C), think, recycle, bottles

1. (B), noodle, salty, need, delicious, sure, where

2. (C), move, apartment, watch, from, disagree, team

3. (C), tell a lie, problem, course, think, worry

1. (C), faster, rush hour

2. (B), learn, not safe, alone

1. (B), wants, zoo, told, museum, should, do

2. (A), put, wood, winter, colder, gather, firewood

UNIT 3

1. (1) scary　(2) ghost　(3) dirty　(4) bright　(5) real　(6) exprience　(7) costume　(8) relax　(9) culture　(10) exciting

2. (1) think of, white bag, think, bright, dirty　(2) believe, ghosts, No, don't, believed, child

3. (1) How do you feel about the weather today?　(2) What is your opinion on studying abroad?

1. (C), believe

2. (D), opinion, weekend

1. (A), feel, movie, very much, cinema, food, far

2. (C), opinion, exercising, walk, think, important, again

3. (A), believe, do, am, aren't, good

1. (C), raising, cat, hamster, allergic

2. (A), about, hairstyle, good

1. (D), What, new bag, birthday, color

2. (B), famous, think, opinion

TOSEL 실전문제 4　1. (A)　2. (B)　3. (D)　4. (C)　5. (B)

CHAPTER 5										p.128

UNIT 1
Practice
p.131

1. (1) kind (2) carry (3) heavy (4) lend (5) need (6) handle (7) own (8) on my own (9) give a hand (10) bread

2. (1) Excuse, could, help, Sure, problem, carry   (2) Why, don't, classroom, good, go

3. (1) Can I get you coffee and bread for breakfast?   (2) Would you like me to give you a wake-up call?

Part A
p.132

1. (A), someone, plant, please

2. (D), Could, find, wallet

Part B
p.133

1. (D), get, something, welcome, bad, empty, some

2. (D), plan, birthday, perfect, need, hand, Sure

3. (C), with, homework, answer, busy, yourself, write

Part C
p.134

1. (C), Would, drive, thanks, far, walk

2. (A), use, instead, plastic, helpful, saving

Part D
p.135

1. (B), lend, hand, what, with, hold, door

2. (C), wash, dishes, on, own, always, Let

UNIT 2
Practice
p.139

1. (1) worry (2) upset (3) still (4) promise (5) alright (6) slip (7) everywhere (8) miss (9) look for (10) knee

2. (1) hurt, slipped, floor, bandage   (2) upset, everything, okay, angry, broke, promise

3. (1) We looked for you everywhere.   (2) What is getting you down?

Part A
p.140

1. (D), worried, horse

2. (B), worry, about, presentation

Part B
p.141

1. (C), broke, make, call, call, bag, worried, good

2. (C), hit, head, front, busy, sorry, alright, okay

3. (B), heard, accident, hurt, awful, fine, excited, better

Part C
p.142

1. (D), everything, upset, son, playing, games

2. (C), water, worried, health, drink, water

Part D
p.143

1. (C), wrong, nervous, worried, concert, Everything, going

2. (B), okay, getting, fight, words, don't, sorry

UNIT 3
Practice
p.147

1. (1) invite (2) mind (3) offer (4) plan (5) holiday (6) theater (7) ticket (8) welcome (9) suggestion (10) glad

2. (1) something in mind, book, ticket   (2) suggestion, tonight, would, like

3. (1) Sure, I'll be there on time.   (2) We are throwing a party tonight for the new teammate.

Part A
p.148

1. (C), join, soccer

2. (B), Why, take, picture

Part B
p.149

1. (C), something, drink, empty, coffee, tea, please

2. (A), Would, stay, love, on time, inviting, mind

3. (D), decide, menu, asked, never, suggestion, suggestion

Part C
p.150

1. (A), caught, cold, What, How, doctor

2. (C), basketball, us, offer, guitar, lesson

Part D
p.151

1. (A), camping, this, very, busy, how, next

2. (B), buy, give, something, mind, idea, perfume

TOSEL 실전문제 5   1. (C)   2. (B)   3. (D)   4. (A)   5. (C)

CHAPTER 6

UNIT 1		
Practice p.159	🔊	1. (1) mess (2) bin (3) bark (4) strict (5) garbage (6) reduce (7) trash (8) surprise (9) pollution (10) monster
	🔊	2. (1) told, birthday, Friday, throw, surprise (2) tell, meeting, afternoon
	🔊	3. (1) Did you hear the news about the new English teacher? (2) We will talk about how to reduce pollution.
Part A p.160	✏	1. (A), mother, carrots, eyes
	✏	2. (B), talk, how, electricity
Part B p.161	✏	1. (C), topic, presentation, very well, going to, role model, end
	✏	2. (D), Will, tell, nothing, When, begins, way
	✏	3. (A), know, broke up, listen, exciting, leave, answer
Part C p.162	✏	1. (C), told, shooting, stars, bring, jacket
	✏	2. (B), getting, married, know, wedding, June
Part D p.163	✏	1. (A), speaking, test, made, mistakes, too, will, parents
	✏	2. (C), call for, did, about, trip, forgot, yesterday
UNIT 2		
Practice p.167	🔊	1. (1) truth (2) happen (3) honest (4) quiet (5) mistake (6) nothing (7) anything (8) present (9) check (10) finish
	🔊	2. (1) like, present, truth (2) Were, busy, honest, finish
	🔊	3. (1) What do you think of my new dress? (2) John, can you tell me what really happend?
Part A p.168	✏	1. (A), honest, ate, pie
	✏	2. (D), Truthfully, fishing, friends
Part B p.169	✏	1. (D), copy, essay, photocopied, mistake, bring, forgot
	✏	2. (C), think, hairstyle, cute, money, look, before
	✏	3. (D), ready, exam, homework, spent, lost, at all
Part C p.170	✏	1. (B), happened, diary, truth, little, ripped
	✏	2. (D), fantastic, character, honest, really, action
Part D p.171	✏	1. (C), happy, face, finished, writing, truth, due
	✏	2. (C), over, together, science, fun, understand, lesson
UNIT 3		
Practice p.175	🔊	1. (1) vacation (2) travel abroad (3) fly (4) visit (5) stay (6) safe (7) due (8) extra (9) plenty (10) volleyball
	🔊	2. (1) due, assignment, plenty, time (2) bag, beneath, desk
	🔊	3. (1) Do you have plans for the winter vacation? (2) What do I need to bring to camp?
Part A p.176	✏	1. (C), fox, on
	✏	2. (C), plan, vacation, tennis
Part B p.177	✏	1. (A), due, project, due, come, project, finised
	✏	2. (C), often, cycling, seafood, Every, often, second, takes, fly
	✏	3. (C), long, stay, stay, save, staying, took, hours
Part C p.178	✏	1. (C), bring, lesson, Wear, suit, cap
	✏	2. (D), New Year's Day, see, sunrise, mountain
Part D p.179	✏	1. (C), date, group, next, Tuesday, speed, file
	✏	2. (B), know, date, told, July, bring, present

TOSEL 실전문제 6	1. (D)	2. (A)	3. (B)	4. (D)	5. (C)

UNIT 1
◆ Practice
p.187

1. (1) have to   (2) library   (3) action   (4) chores   (5) allow   (6) rule   (7) instruction   (8) hallway   (9) forget   (10) copy

2. (1) write, down, shouldn't, copy   (2) have, dinner, need, walk

3. (1) No, you have to do some house chores.   (2) Don't forget to do your dishes before going out.

◆ Part A
p.188

1. (C), leave, off, lights

2. (B), pictures, museum

◆ Part B
p.189

1. (B), Be, careful, standing, kind, know, follow, every day

2. (C), outside, play, later, need to, have to, practice

3. (C), forget, before, Sure, forgot, worry, already

◆ Part C
p.190

1. (A), mess, need, to, dishes, floor

2. (C), ordered, piece, Wash, first, bring

◆ Part D
p.191

1. (D), Where, feeling, cinema, leave, Why, coming

2. (C), rules, follow, copy, answer, right, more

UNIT 2
◆ Practice
p.195

1. (1) lights   (2) safety   (3) careful   (4) attention   (5) road   (6) jaywalking   (7) helmet   (8) cross   (9) bike   (10) place

2. (1) inside, box, careful, souvenir   (2) homework, later, If, were

3. (1) Pay attention to the road when you are driving.   (2) Be careful when you cross the road.

◆ Part A
p.196

1. (C), Watch, wild, road

2. (B), careful, floor

◆ Part B
p.197

1. (D), moblie, phone, phone, Make sure, anything, with

2. (D), too, get, boiling, toys, mad, cameras

3. (C), sandwich, fridge, go, do, eat, write

◆ Part C
p.198

1. (D), shopping, size, try, different

2. (B), pizza, about, health, were, whole

◆ Part D
p.199

1. (D), hand, box, and, carry, heavy, inside

2. (B), remember, exercise, forgot, start, should, attention

UNIT 3
◆ Practice
p.203

1. (1) learn   (2) disapp-ointed   (3) fold   (4) dessert   (5) fair   (6) finish   (7) quickly   (8) nap   (9) noise   (10) yell

2. (1) tell, rules, talking, yelling   (2) do, shouldn't, finishing

3. (1) You shouldn't eat your food so quickly.   (2) What did I say about the noise level?

◆ Part A
p.204

1. (B), feet, desk

2. (A), keep, elbows, off

◆ Part B
p.205

1. (D), think, heels, yell, attention, gloves, heels

2. (B), piece, chocolate, coffee, snacks, chocolate, already

3. (A), table, manners, walk, wait, close, wash

◆ Part C
p.206

1. (D), think, cold, ice cream, until, better

2. (D), teacher, museum, talk, phone, museum

◆ Part D
p.207

1. (D), sorry, being, coming, again, called, needed

2. (C), yours, steal, pretty, put, disappointed, return

TOSEL 실전문제 7   1. (B)   2. (D)   3. (A)   4. (C)   5. (A)

UNIT 1 Practice p.215	🔊	1. (1) instead (2) order (3) sale (4) extra (5) mall (6) meal (7) vegetarian (8) aisle (9) restaurant (10) delicious
	🔊	2. (1) where, find, aisle, beverages (2) electronic, devices, How, much
	🔊	3. (1) I would like a cheese burger with extra tomatoes, please. (2) Excuse me, I am looking for a vegetarian restaurant.
Part A p.216	✏	1. (D), would, spaghetti, tomato
	✏	2. (B), looking for, striped
Part B p.217	✏	1. (D), have, shopping, second, mall, call, oil
	✏	2. (D), where, stationary, close, yesterday, pencil case, next to
	✏	3. (A), try, on, need, bigger, cheese, counter
Part C p.218	✏	1. (A), get, card, notebook, pay, Cash
	✏	2. (B), earphones, electronic, sale, where, electronics
Part D p.219	✏	1. (C), shoes, popular, style, these, brand, product
	✏	2. (B), want, help, looking, cleaner, item, sale
UNIT 2 Practice p.223	🔊	1. (1) lost (2) block (3) quickest (4) take (5) pass (6) aquarium (7) pharmacy (8) gas station (9) cross (10) kind
	🔊	2. (1) where, field, Cross, beside (2) pharmacy, right, left
	🔊	3. (1) Take the bus at Union station. (2) Could you help me please? I'm looking for a bank.
Part A p.224	✏	1. (A), Could, police station
	✏	2. (C), the nearest bank
Part B p.225	✏	1. (A), bus stop, near, corner, Turn off, bridge, walked up
	✏	2. (B), best, around, mornings, subway, around, get off
	✏	3. (D), where, Museum, by, museum, along, blocks
Part C p.226	✏	1. (D), please, looking for, block, next to
	✏	2. (D), Airport, here, quickest , shuttle bus
Part D p.227	✏	1. (A), miss, train, ticket, left, quickest, station
	✏	2. (D), Pardon me, far, bakery, in front of
UNIT 3 Practice p.231	🔊	1. (1) happen (2) noise (3) escape (4) tasty (5) drill (6) suddenly (7) festival (8) neighbor (9) cotton candy (10) sleepy
	🔊	2. (1) hear, fire, university, set, fire (2) festival, cotton, watched, parade
	🔊	3. (1) What's going on here? (2) What happened yesterday night?
Part A p.232	✏	1. (A), accident, road
	✏	2. (D), hacked, computer
Part B p.233	✏	1. (C), happened, to, fast, early, fell down, stand on
	✏	2. (B), set fire, office, going, reason, were, wrong
	✏	3. (B), window, broken, stay, happen, have, often
Part C p.234	✏	1. (D), between, fight, money
	✏	2. (C), lost, kitten, must
Part D p.235	✏	1. (C), going on, anything, car racing, explain
	✏	2. (D), that, hit, How, happen, jaywalked, street
TOSEL 실전문제 8		1. (B) 2. (A) 3. (D) 4. (A) 5. (C)

memo

memo

memo